NOWHERE IS A PLACE
TRAVELS IN PATAGONIA

Bruce Chatwin AND Paul Theroux

PHOTOGRAPHS BY Jeff Gnass

INTRODUCTION BY Paul Theroux

A YOLLA BOLLY PRESS BOOK PUBLISHED BY

Sierra Club Books

SAN FRANCISCO

A YOLLA BOLLY PRESS BOOK

This book was produced in association with the publisher at The Yolla Bolly Press, Covelo, California, under the supervision of James Robertson and Carolyn Robertson, with assistance from Diana Fairbanks and Renee Menge. Composition by Wilsted & Taylor, Oakland, California.

The Sierra Club, founded in 1892 by John Muir, has devoted itself to the study and protection of the earth's scenic and ecological resources—mountains, wetlands, woodlands, wild shores and rivers, deserts and plains. The publishing program of the Sierra Club offers books to the public as a nonprofit educational service in the hope that they may enlarge the public's understanding of the Club's basic concerns. The point of view expressed in each book, however, does not necessarily represent that of the Club. The Sierra Club has some sixty chapters coast to coast, in Canada, Hawaii, and Alaska. For information about how you may participate in its programs to preserve wilderness and the quality of life, please address inquiries to Sierra Club, 730 Polk Street, San Francisco, CA 94109.

LIBRARY OF CONGRESS CATALOGING-IN-PUBLICATION DATA

Chatwin, Bruce, 1940–1989.
  [Patagonia revisited]
  Nowhere is a place : travels in Patagonia / text by Bruce Chatwin and Paul Theroux ; photographs by Jeff Gnass.
    p. cm.
  Originally published as: Patagonia revisited. Salisbury, Wiltshire : Michael Russell, 1985. With new frwd. and photos.
  Lecture presented by the authors at the Royal Geographical Society Hall in London.
  Includes bibliographical references
  ISBN 0-87156-500-5
  1. Patagonia (Argentina and Chile)—Description and travel.   2. Patagonia (Argentina and Chile) in literature. 3. Chatwin, Bruce, 1940–1989—Journeys—Patagonia (Argentina and Chile)   4. Theroux, Paul—Journeys— Patagonia (Argentina and Chile)   I. Theroux, Paul. II. Gnass, Jeff.   III. Title.
F2936.C473   1992
918.2'7046—dc20   91-46287
                                    CIP

Printed and bound by Dai Nippon Printing Co. (Hong Kong), Ltd.

10 9 8 7 6 5 4 3 2 1

CONTENTS

CHATWIN REVISITED

WHEN I THINK of Bruce Chatwin, who was my friend, I am always reminded of a particular night, a dinner at the Royal Geographical Society, hearing him speaking animatedly about various high mountains he had climbed. And that struck me as very odd, because I knew he had never been much of a mountaineer.

I was some way down the table but I heard him clearly. He spoke in his usual way, very rapidly and insistently, stuttering and interrupting and laughing, until he had commanded enough attention to begin speechifying. Being Chatwin, he did not stop at the peaks he scaled. He had plans for further assaults and expeditions—all of them one-man affairs, no oxygen, minimum equipment, rush the summit—and as he appeared to be holding his listeners spellbound (they were murmuring, "Of course" and "Extraordinary" and "Quite right"), I peeked over to see their faces. On Chatwin's right was Chris Bonington, conqueror of Nanga Parbat and numerous other twenty-thousand footers, and on his left, Lord Hunt, leader of the first successful expedition up Everest.

"Chatter, chatter, chatter, Chatwin," a mutual friend once said to me. He was smiling, but you could tell his head still hurt. Bruce had just been his houseguest for a week. "He simply never stops."

This talking was the most striking thing about him, yet there were so many other aspects of him that made an immediate impression. He was handsome, he had piercing eyes, he was very quick—full of nervous gestures—a rapid walker, often surprisingly mocking of the English. Of course, Bruce talks a lot, people said. It's because he's alone so much of the time. It was true that he was intensely solitary—he was given to sudden disappearances, that is, and everyone assumed he was alone. But even so, I believed he talked to himself, probably yakked nonstop, rehearsing his stories and practicing funny accents and mimicry: it is a habit of many writers and travelers. I am sorry I never asked him whether he did this. I am sure he would have let out his screeching laugh and said, "Constantly!"

He was such a darter he seldom stayed still long enough for anyone to sum him up, but when he died many people published their memories of him—and the portraits were so different. It was amazing how many people, old and young, many of them distinguished, a number of them glamorous, gathered to mourn him, in a Greek Orthodox Church in London. Salman Rushdie sat in the pew in front of me with his then wife. It was Valentine's Day, 1989, the day after the Ayatollah condemned Salman to death—I thought it was a hollow condemnation, and I joked about it. Judging from the congregation, Bruce had known everyone in London. But he had flitted from one to another, keeping them separate, making a point of not introducing them, but often dropping their names.

He did not just drop Francis Bacon's name, he went one better and mimicked him—which suggested how well he knew him: "Oh, dear," he would say, with an epicene hiss, "a million quid for one of my paintings— I'll just spend it on champagne." He could get two or three boasts into a single statement, as in "Werner Herzog and I just hiked two hundred miles in Dahomey" or "David Hockney told me that his favorite painter is Liotard, a seventeenth-century Swiss. He's brilliant. I often go to the Rijksmuseum just to look at his work." (This must have been true, because one day in Amsterdam Bruce showed me a Liotard painting.)

Postcards are the preferred medium for many self-advertisers, combining vividness, cheapness and an economy of effort—something like a miniature billboard. Bruce was a great sender of postcards. He sent them to me from France, from China, from Australia and from the artists' colony Yaddo. *Feverish lesbian sculptors doing vulvaic iconography in plastic,* he wrote from Yaddo. He encapsulated a theory about an Italian writer in Yunnan. From Australia he wrote, *You must come here. The men are awful, like bits of cardboard, but the women are splendid.* And on another postcard (this one of a bushranger), *Have become interested in an extreme situation—of Spanish monks in an Aborig-*

inal mission and am about to start sketching an outline. Anyway the crisis of the 'shall-never-write-another-line' sort is now over.

In terms of writing he was in a state of permanent crisis. Perhaps he had started to write too late in his life, perhaps he lacked confidence. A writer talking to another writer about the difficulty of writing is hardly riveting—you just want to go away. Bruce was at his least interesting bemoaning his writer's block, and I often felt that he was not really bemoaning it at all, but rather boasting about the subtlety of his special gift, and his implication was of it being so finely tuned it occasionally emitted a high-pitched squeal and seemed to go dead; but no, it was still pulsing like a laser—it had simply drifted an instant from his target. I had no such story to tell—I was producing a book a year, turning the big wooden crank on my chomping meatgrinder. How could I talk about a literary crisis, when all I had to do to continue was grab the crank and give it a spin?

He did write like an angel most of the time, but he is never more Chatwinesque than when he is yielding to his conceit. In *The Songlines* he mentions how he happened to be in Vienna speaking with Konrad Lorenz (in itself something of a boast) on the subject of aggression. Considering that Lorenz was the author of *On Aggression*, this was audacious of Bruce; but he was unfazed in the presence of the master, and went further, cheerfully adumbrating his own theories of aggression, with much the same verve as he described his mountaineering exploits to Lord Hunt.

"'But surely,' I persisted, 'haven't we got the concepts of "aggression" and "defense" mixed up?'" Bruce asks pointedly, implying that Konrad Lorenz has been barking up the wrong tree in sixty-odd years of scientific research. Bruce then sketches his Beast Theory: mankind needing to see his enemy as a beast in order to overcome him; or needing to be a "surrogate beast" in order to see men as prey.

It seems astonishing that the world renowned zoologist and philosopher did not find Bruce's theory conventional and obvious (as it sounds to me). Instead, "Lorenz tugged at his beard, gave me a searching look and said, ironically or not I'll never know: 'What you have just said is totally new.'"

Chatwin claimed to have the usual English disdain for flattery and praise, which is odd, because he adored it, and of course—praise is cheap and plentiful—it was lavished upon him. To need praise is human enough. Bruce solicited it by circulating to his friends bound proof copies of his books. We would read them and scribble remarks in the margin. I remember the scribbled-over copy of *The Viceroy of Ouidah*. My remarks were anodyne, but some other snippets of marginalia were shrieks of derision: "Ha! Ha!" or "Rubbish" or "Impossible!" He said he didn't care. He was at his most unconvincing when he was dismissive of praise.

Here he is in Dahomey, speaking to an African soldier, in his sketch, "A Coup."

"You are English?"

"Yes."

"But you speak an excellent French."

"Passable," I said.

"With a Parisian accent I should have said."

"I have lived in Paris."

Much of his reading was in French, usually obscure books. It would be something like Rousseau's *Des reveries du promeneur solitaire (Reveries of a Solitary Walker)*, Gide's *Nourritures terrestres*, Arthur Rimbaud's *Les illuminations*, or—one of the strangest travel books ever written—Xavier de Maistre's *Voyage au tour de ma chambre (A Trip Around My Room)*. When he found a book that few other people had read he tended to overpraise it. He might dismiss a book precisely because it was popular.

His ability to speak French well was of course part of his gift for mimicry, and it delighted me, though it irritated many who felt Bruce was showing off. When Bruce appeared on the Parisian literary TV show *Apostrophe* he was interviewed in French and he replied with complete fluency, talking a mile a minute.

He was full of theories. One was highly complex and concerned the origin of the color red as the official color of Marxism. This theory took you across the ocean to Uruguay. It involved butchers in Montevideo, peasants on horseback, Garibaldi, and the Colorado Party. I think I've got that right. The theory then whisked you back to Europe, to Italy, to Germany, to Russia and to the adoption of—was it an apron? was it a flag? It was all very confusing, though Chatwin told the story with precision, and always the same way. I know this because I heard him explain the theory at least four times. He told it to everyone. It was tiresome to hear this theory repeated, but it was even more annoying to realize that he had not remembered that he had told you before.

That was something his friends had to endure. If he couldn't recall that he was repeating something to you verbatim—shrieking each predictable thing and looking eager and hopeful—that seemed to indicate that he cared more about the monologuing itself than about you. The worst aspect of monologuists is their impartiality, their utter lack of interest in whoever they happen to be drilling into. Because it hardly matters who they are with, they victimize everyone, great and small.

Bruce was a fairly bad listener. If you told him something he would quickly say that he knew it already, and he would go on talking. Usually he was such a good talker that it hardly mattered.

But while most of us knew his stories, there were always great gaps in between them. There is an English quip to express befuddlement, *Who's he when he's at home?* Exactly. Everyone knew Bruce was married—we had met his wife, Elizabeth. But what sort of marriage was this? "A *marriage blanche,*" a friend once said to me, pursing his lips. Bruce was in his way devoted to his wife, but the very fact of Bruce having a wife was so improbable that no one quite believed it.

One night at dinner, just before he left the table I heard Bruce distinctly speak of his plans for the near future and say, "I'm going to meet my wife in Tibet." Afterwards, one of the people present said, "Did he say his wife was dead?" and another replied, "No. He said his wife's in bed."

He kept so much to himself. We heard the colorful stories of a born raconteur. But what of the rest of it? We wondered what his private life was really like, and sometimes we speculated. His first book, *In Patagonia,* embodied all his faults and virtues. It was highly original, courageous, and vividly written. He inscribed a copy to me, writing generously, *To Paul Theroux, who unwittingly triggered this off* (and he explained that a book of mine had inspired him). But his book was full of gaps. How had he traveled from here to there? How had he met this or that person? Life was never so neat as Bruce made out. What of the other, small, telling details, which to me gave a book reality?

I used to look for links between the chapters, and between two conversations or pieces of geography. Why hadn't he put them in?

"Why do you think it matters?" he said to me.

"Because it's interesting," I said. "And because I think when you're writing a travel book you have to come clean."

This made him laugh, and then he said something that I have always taken to be a pronouncement that was very near to being his motto. He said—he screeched—"I don't believe in coming clean!"

We had a mutual friend, an older and distinguished writer who felt that Bruce was trying to live down the shame of being the son of a Birmingham lawyer. I challenged this.

The man said, "No. You're wrong. Look at Noel Coward. His mother kept a lodging house. And he pretended to be so grand—that theatrical English accent. All that posturing. He knew he was common. It was all a pretense. Think of his pain."

This might have been true in a small way of Bruce, but I think that he was secretive by nature. It kept him aloof. It helped him in his flitting around. He never revealed himself totally to anyone, as far as I know, and in this way he kept his personality intact. In any case, he never struck me as being thoroughly English. He was more cosmopolitan—liking France, feeling liberated in America, being fascinated by Russia and China, something of a cultural exile.

I am skirting the subject of his sexual preference because it does not seem to me that it should matter. Yet it was obvious to anyone who knew him that in speaking tenderly of marital bliss he was always suppressing a secret and more lively belief in homosexuality. That he was homosexual bothered no one; that he never spoke about it was rather disturbing.

In an ungracious memoir, the writer David Plante refused to see Bruce's sense of fun and perhaps even deeper sense of insecurity. Plante wrote at length about how they had gone to a gay disco in London called "Heaven," but it is characteristic of the memoir's dark hints and hypocrisy that Bruce's behavior is regarded as sneaky and insincere, while Plante himself never discloses his own motive for going to the gay hangout.

I wanted to know more about his homosexual life, not because I am prurient but because if I like someone I want to know everything. And while Bruce was secretive himself, he was exasperated by others who kept their secrets. He never wrote about his sexuality, and some of us have laid our souls bare.

When he called me he always did so out of the blue. I liked that. I liked the suddenness of it—it suited my life and my writing. I hated making plans for the future. I might not be in the mood that faroff day, I might be trying to write something. If he called in the morning it was always a proposal to meet that afternoon or evening. And then I might not hear from him for six months or a year.

It surprised me that he had agreed to give a lecture for the Royal Geographical Society, but he had done it on one condition—that it be a duet. Would I agree? I said okay, and I quickly realized we were both doing it so as to seem respectable among all these distinguished explorers and travelers.

Working together with him to prepare the lecture, "Patagonia Revisited," the text of which is the basis of this book, I realized how little I knew him and what an odd fish he was. He was insecure, I knew that, it had the effect of making him seem domineering. "I can't believe you haven't read Pigafetta," he would say, and he would put the book in my hand and insist I read it by tomorrow—and the next day he would say, "Our talk's going to be awful, it's hopeless, I don't know why we agreed to do this," and later on would say, "By the way I've invited the Duke and Duchess of Westminster."

I found this maddening. I felt it was a task we had to perform, and that we would do it well if we were decently prepared. Bruce's moods ranged from rather tiresome high spirits to days of belittling gloom. "No one's going to come," he said. "I'm certainly not inviting anyone."

We got in touch with a dozen members of the RGS who had photographs of Patagonia, and we assembled eighty or a hundred beautiful pictures of the plains, of glaciers, of penguins, of snow and storms.

When the day came it turned out that Bruce had invited many people, including his parents—his big beefy-faced father had the look of a Dickensian solicitor—and he was miffed that the Duke and Duchess hadn't been able to make it. The lecture itself I thought was splendid—not so much for the text but for the atmosphere, the oddity. We gave it in the wooden amphitheater, where so many distinguished explorers had reported back to the society; and we stood in the dark—a little light shining on our notes, while big beautiful pictures of Patagonia flashed on the screen behind us. This was thrilling—just our voices and these vivid Patagonian sights.

There was loud applause afterwards. Bruce, who would have been a wonderful actor, was flushed with pleasure. He had been brilliant, and I realized that he had needed me to encourage him and get him through it.

And when I heard him at dinner regaling Lord Hunt and Chris Bonington with his mountaineering exploits I thought: He's flying!

He traveled. We ran into each other in various places—in America, in Amsterdam. When he wanted to meet someone I knew well he simply asked me to introduce him. Graham Greene he particularly wanted to meet. But Bruce was disappointed. He thought Greene was gaga. He could not understand the mystique. He loved Borges. Later he needed glamour. He let himself be courted by Robert Mapplethorpe. He liked the thought of his portrait appearing in Mapplethorpe's notorious exhibition, along with photographs of women weight-lifters and strange flowers and even stranger sexual practices.

He went to China—just a magazine assignment, but Bruce made it seem as though he had been sent on an expedition by the Royal Geographical Society. I admired that in him. He took his writing assignments seriously, no matter who he was writing for. He was the opposite of a hack, which is to say something of a pedant, but a likable one, who was fastidious and truly knowledgeable.

When he fell deathly ill soon after his China trip the word spread that he had been bitten by a fruit bat in Yunnan and contracted a rare blood disease. Only two other people in the entire world had ever had it, so the story went, and both had died. Bruce was near death, but he fought back and survived. And he had another story to tell at dinner parties—of being bitten by a

Chinese bat. He recovered. A friend said to me, "I just saw Bruce walking through Eaton Square carrying a white truffle."

But the blood disease returned. "I was warned that it might pop up again," Bruce explained. What kind of bat was this exactly? Bruce was vague, and he became very ill. Seeing him was like looking at the sunken cheeks and wasted flesh of a castaway. That image came to me again and again, the image of an abandoned traveler—the worst fate for travelers is that they become lost and instead of revelling in oblivion, they fret and fall ill.

When I visited and revisited his bedroom in Oxfordshire—a pretty, homely farmhouse that Elizabeth kept ticking over, and she also raised sheep—his hands would fly to his face, covering his hollow cheeks.

"God, you're healthy," he would say sadly. But later he would cheer up, making plans. "I'm going to Arizona to see Lisa Lyon. She's fabulous. The woman weight-lifter? You'd love her." And when I prepared to go, he would say, "I'm not ready for *The Tibetan Book of the Dead* yet."

"He expected to get better, and when he got worse he was demoralized and just let go," Elizabeth told me. "He was in terrible pain, but at the height of it he lapsed into a coma, and that was almost a blessing."

Hovering in this fragile state of health he died suddenly. He had been handsome, calculating, and demanding; he was famous for his disappearances. His death was like that, just as sudden, like Bruce on another journey. We were used to his vanishings—his silences could be as conspicuous as his talk. It seems strange, but not unlike him, that he has been gone so long.

PAUL THEROUX

17

NOWHERE IS A PLACE

BRUCE CHATWIN Since its discovery by Magellan in 1520, Patagonia was known as a country of black fogs and whirlwinds at the end of the habited world. The word 'Patagonia', like Mandalay or Timbuctoo, lodged itself in the Western imagination as a metaphor for The Ultimate, the point beyond which one could not go. Indeed, in the opening chapter of *Moby Dick*, Melville uses 'Patagonian' as an adjective for the outlandish, the monstrous and fatally attractive:

> Then the wild and distant seas where he rolled his island bulk; the undeliverable, nameless perils of the whale: these, with all the attending marvels of a thousand Patagonian sights and sounds, helped sway me to my wish.

Paul and I went to Patagonia for very different reasons. But if we are travellers at all, we are literary travellers. A literary reference or connection is likely to excite us as much as a rare animal or plant; and so we touch on some of the instances in which Patagonia has affected the literary imagination.

We are also both fascinated by exiles. If the rest of the world blew up tomorrow, you would still find in Patagonia an astonishing cross-section of the world's nationalities, all of whom have drifted towards these 'final capes of exile' for no other apparent reason than the fact that they were there.

On any one day in Patagonia, the traveller could expect to encounter a Welshman, an English gentleman-farmer, a Haight-Ashbury Flower Child, a Montenegran nationalist, an Afrikaaner, a Persian missionary for the Bahai religion, or the Archdeacon of Buenos Aires on his round of Anglican baptisms.

Or there would be characters like Bautista Dias Low, a horse-tamer and Anarchist, whom I met near Puerto Natales in Southern Chile; and who, with his own hands, had hacked himself a cattle ranch from

OPPOSITE Dawn casts its spell on the pampa east of Macizo del Fitzroy, Argentina.

the rain forest. He surprised me with some intricate knowledge about the voyage of the *Beagle*: not that he had read books about it, or could even read, but because his great-grandfather, Captain William Low, had been Darwin and FitzRoy's pilot through the *canales*. It was generous of him to attribute his courage and absolute bloody-mindedness to his *sangre británica*.

The earliest travellers to Patagonia definitely mistook it for the Land of the Devil. For one, the mainland was inhabited by a race of giants—the Tehuelche Indians, who turned out, on closer acquaintance, to be less gigantic and less fierce than their reputation—and may indeed have given Swift his model for the coarse but amiable inhabitants of Brobdingnag.

Patagonia was also a land of strange beasts and birds. 'Pen-gwyn' is thought to be a Welsh expression for 'flightless bird'; the Elizabethan sailors had a superstition that jackass penguins were the souls of their drowned comrades; and, in the seventeenth century, Sir John Narborough, visiting Puerto Deseado, described them as 'standing upright like little children in white aprons in company together'. There was the condor, which somehow got confused with Zeus's eagle and Sinbad the Sailor's roc; and it was off the coast of Tierra del Fuego that Captain Shelvocke, an eighteenth-century English privateer, saw an albatross:

The heavens were perpetually hid from us by gloomy dismal clouds . . . one would think it impossible that any living thing could subsist in so rigid a climate; and, indeed . . . we had not had the sight of one fish of any kind . . . nor one sea-bird, except a disconsolate black *albitross* . . . hovering about us as if he had lost himself, till *Hatley* (my second Captain) observing, in one of his

OPPOSITE Spring wildflowers crowd around glacial erratics on foothills below Fitzroy, Argentina.

22

melancholy fits, that this bird was always hovering near us, imagined, from his colour, that it might be some ill omen . . . [and] after some fruitless attempts, at length, shot the *Albitross*, not doubting (perhaps) that we should have a fair wind after it. . . .

This text, of course, read first by Wordsworth and passed on to Coleridge, became:

> 'In mist or cloud, on mast or shroud,
> It perched for vespers nine;
> Whiles all the night, through fog-smoke white,
> Glimmered the white Moon-shine.'
>
> 'God save thee, ancient Mariner!
> From the fiends, that plague thee thus!—
> Why look'st thou so?'—'With my cross-bow
> I shot the Albatross.'*

Nor did the later nineteenth century do anything to dispel the idea that Patagonia was a Land of Marvels. The moment scientists, such as Darwin, scratched the soil, they found it to be a boneyard of prehistoric mammals, some of which were thought to be alive. They also found petrified forests, fizzling lakes, and glaciers of blue ice sliding through forests of southern beech.

PAUL THEROUX When I think of going anywhere, I think of going south. I associate the word 'south' with freedom, and at a very young age I bought Sir Ernest Shackleton's book *South* for the title alone. My first job was in the southern part of Nyasaland, and it wasn't a bad choice: there I could think straight, and began for the first time in my life to write.

OPPOSITE Badlands overlook Río La Leona on the pampa, Argentina.

*Since we gave the lecture, another fatal shooting took place in these waters— the sinking of the Argentine cruiser *Belgrano* by a British submarine on 2 May 1982. A day or so later, a journalist commented that this action would prove to be 'Mrs Thatcher's albatross' without, perhaps, being aware of the literary reverberations. The mate Hatley shot his bird just after the ship had rounded the easternmost cape of Tierra del Fuego; the *Belgrano* was outside the war zone, heading back towards Tierra del Fuego when the torpedoes hit.

25

ABOVE Conch shell on cracked tidal mud at Río Coig on the Atlantic coast, Argentina.

OPPOSITE Late afternoon shadows emphasize the wind's signature on sand dunes near Lago Argentino, Argentina.

I had nothing to do, so I decided to go to Patagonia. It was an easy choice. I knew it was the emptiest part of America and one of the least known—consequently a forcing-house of legends, half-truths and misinformation. And it was reachable by land. There is no greater pleasure than waking in the morning in Boston and knowing that you are to travel 15,000 miles and not have to board an aeroplane. (I was wrong about that, but I didn't know it at the time.) Patagonia seemed like a precinct of my own country, the people there called themselves Americans. Looking at the map it seemed that by moving south I could pass through Mexico, sprint across Central America and entering the great funnel of South America drop slowly down the Andes and roll naturally into Patagonia, where I would come to rest. It was snowing in Boston when I left: Patagonia promised a different climate, a change of mood, and complete freedom to wander.

That is the best mood to have when starting out. I was willing, I was game; it is only later, in travel, that one understands that the greatest distance inspires the greatest illusions, and that solitary travel is both a pleasure and a penalty.

Patagonia has not been widely photographed. I had no mental image of it, only the fanciful blur of legend, the giants on the shore, the ostrich on the plain, and a sense of displaced people, like my own ancestors who had fled from Europe. When I tried to call up an image of Patagonia, nothing came and I was as helpless as if I had tried to describe the landscape of a distant planet or paint the smell of an onion. The unknown landscape is justification enough for going to it.

My other reason was plainer. In 1901, my great-grandfather left Italy for Argentina. He was fifty-two and had had a fairly miserable life, farming in a small village called Agazzano, near Piacenza. Argentina was America, an *estancia*, a better life; he had four children. He knew what he was in for—other Italians had gone and sent back

reports that it was a good place for Italians to settle. Indeed, there were so many Italians there that W. H. Hudson was convinced that the place was spoiled forever—one of his reasons for not ever going back to Argentina was that the Italians had interfered with the bird life.

Anyway, this man Francesco Calesa packed his bags for Argentina. He was not unusual. Thousands were doing the same. But when he got to the boat he was told that there had been an outbreak of yellow fever in Buenos Aires, no one could go to Argentina, and the ship was re-routed to New York. With some misgivings, Calesa, with his wife and four children, went to New York. He hated New York at once, and from the moment of his arrival plotted his escape. But his wife wouldn't go, and when Calesa finally fled America, the marriage was fractured, Calesa was alone and ageing and no longer confident enough to start again in Argentina.

So Patagonia was the promise of an unknown landscape, the experience of freedom, the most southerly part of my own country, the perfect destination; but it was also a way of completing the trip my great-grandfather had wanted to make.

And when, after the long trip, I arrived in Patagonia I felt I was nowhere. But the most surprising thing of all was that I was still in the world—I had been travelling south for months. The landscape had a gaunt expression, but I could not deny that it had readable features and that I existed in it. This was a discovery—the look of it. I thought: *Nowhere is a place.*

Down there the Patagonian valley deepened to grey rock, wearing its aeons' stripes and split by floods. Ahead, there was a succession of hills, whittled and fissured by the wind, which now sang in the bushes. The bushes shook with this song. They stiffened again and were silent. The sky was clear blue. A puff of cloud, white as a quince

OPPOSITE Moraine ridges and talus boulders in a cirque below Monte Almirante Nieto, Chile.

flower, carried a small shadow from town, or from the South Pole. I saw it approach. It rippled across the bushes and passed over me, a brief chill, and then it went rucking east. There were no voices here. There was this, what I saw; and though beyond it were mountains and glaciers and albatrosses and Indians, there was nothing here to speak of, nothing to delay me further. Only the Patagonian paradox: tiny blossoms in vast space; to be here, it helped to be a miniaturist, or else interested in enormous empty spaces. There was no intermediate zone of study. Either the enormity of the desert or the sight of a tiny flower. In Patagonia you had to choose between the tiny or the vast.

BRUCE CHATWIN For me, Patagonia was a Land of Marvels from the precocious age of three. In my grandmother's cabinet of curiosities there was a piece of animal's skin with coarse reddish hair, stuck to a card with a rusty pin.

'What's that?' I asked, and was told: 'A piece of brontosaurus'—or at least, that is what I thought I was told.

The story, as I knew it, was that my grandmother's cousin, Charley Milward the Sailor, had found a brontosaurus perfectly preserved in a glacier in Tierra del Fuego. He had it salted, packed in barrels and sent to the Natural History Museum in South Kensington. Unfortunately, though, it went rotten on its voyage through the tropics, and that was why you saw a brontosaurus skeleton in the Museum, but no skin. He had, however, sent a little piece to my grandmother, by post.

The story, of course, was untrue; and it was a terrible blow, at the age of nine or so, to learn that brontosauruses had no hair, but scaly, armoured hide. The beast of my childhood dreams turned out, in fact, to be the mylodon, or giant sloth*—an animal that died out in

OPPOSITE Morning clouds mingle with Torre Central and Torre Norte above a forested ridge, Chile.

*Bones of the mylodon were found by Darwin at Punta Alta. See Alan Moorehead, *Darwin and the Beagle*, pp. 82–87.

Patagonia about 10,000 years ago, but whose skin, bones and excrement were found, conserved by dryness and salt, in a cave at Last Hope Sound, in the Chilean province of Magallanes.

My cousin Charley was an eccentric, somewhat peppery captain of the New Zealand Shipping Company, whose first command, the *Mataura*, got wrecked on Desolation Island, at the entrance to the Strait of Magellan, in 1898. While salvaging the wreck, he succumbed to the lure of the Far South and settled in the gloomy port of Punta Arenas, where he bought a share in an iron foundry. In 1904 he became British Consul, and when he came to build a house, he reconstructed, out of homesickness, his father's parsonage in Birmingham: the neighbours used to say, 'I suppose he thinks he'll go to Heaven quicker in a place like that.' It was in this house, in 1915, that Sir Ernest Shackleton stayed during those terrible days waiting for the Chilean Navy to send its tug, the *Yelcho*, to fetch his men off Elephant Island.

Twelve years before that, however, Charley had helped a half-mad German gold-panner called Albert Konrad to dynamite the cave for mylodon skin and bones which, by that time, had become a saleable commodity to the natural history museums of Europe. Some zoologists, including Sir Arthur Smith Woodward, had thought the beast was still alive, and the *Daily Express* financed an expedition to find it. They failed, of course, but the episode left its mark on literature, in that it seems to have been an ingredient of Conan Doyle's *The Lost World*.

Never have I wanted anything as I wanted that piece of skin. But when my grandmother died, it got thrown away, and I vowed that, one day, I would go and find a replacement. This spurious quest ended, one stormy afternoon in 1976, when I sat at the back of the cave, after finding a few strands of mylodon hair and a lump of my-

OPPOSITE Wind-shaped grasses on a mountainside overlook icebergs in Lago Grey, Chile.

lodon dung, which looked a bit like last week's horse (so much so that my cleaning lady took exception to it and, the other day, chucked it out). At the moment of discovery I heard voices chanting, 'Ave Maria!'—and thought I'd definitely gone mad. The singers were the nuns from a convent in Punta Arenas on their Saturday afternoon bus tour. I had already seen them, the week before, on another visit, at the penguin colony on Cabo Virgines.

My piece of dung wasn't exactly the Golden Fleece, but it did give me the idea for the form of a travel book, for the oldest kind of traveller's tale is one in which the narrator leaves home and goes to a far country in search of a legendary beast.

PAUL THEROUX Within a few years of Darwin's visit (1832) to Patagonia, an American family migrated to Argentina and settled in the Río de la Plata region, about ten miles from Buenos Aires. They were among the first Americans there, and they were Yankees to the core: the man was born in the Massachusetts seaport of Marblehead, his wife—descended from Pilgrim Fathers—was from Maine. They farmed with little success, but remained in Argentina for the rest of their lives. These were the parents of W. H. Hudson, who was born in Quilmes in 1841.

He had a strange pedigree for someone who considered himself English. For thirty-two years he lived in Argentina; he spent one year in Patagonia, around the Río Negro. In 1868 his father died and he left South America and went to England, where he remained, living largely in penury, his wife running one unsuccessful boarding house after another. He died on the top floor of the last boarding house, in North Kensington—in the small room where he had worked. It must have been hell, because he was six foot three.

OPPOSITE Spires and summits of Cerro Torre and Macizo del Fitzroy light up at sunrise, Argentina.

He appears to have been the serenest man imaginable: he never forgot Patagonia and never stopped writing about it. What he sought in England was its Patagonian-like places—in Cornwall and on Salisbury Plain, the flat, wind-swept and unpeopled districts. He described himself as 'a naturalist in the old, original sense of the word, who is mainly concerned with the "life and conversation of animals"'.

Jorge Luis Borges once said: 'You will find nothing there. There is nothing in Patagonia. That's why Hudson liked it. You will notice there are no people in his books.'

This is partly true, and in *Idle Days in Patagonia* Hudson suggests a reason: 'In spite of what we have been taught, it is sometimes borne in on us that man is a little lower than the brutes.' Hudson's books are peculiar. Some are entirely about birds. One novel, *A Crystal Age*, preaches against the sexual impulse. In this he advances the view that Industrialism, with its uncreative tasks, accentuates the sexual urge; the weakness of man is that he is oversexed. He believed the best recourse was for society to model itself on the beehive, with one woman in a community as the child-bearing queen bee. The central thought, he wrote to Edward Garnett, was that there would be no peace on earth until that sexual 'fury has burnt itself out'. He married at the age of thirty-five; his wife was fifty. They had no children.

The message of *Idle Days in Patagonia*, which was written in a London boarding house in 1893, is in Hudson's own capital letters: TRY PATAGONIA. Patagonia is the cure for mankind's ills. It is also the occasion for a man to see how mistaken Darwin, Melville and Leigh Hunt were in their various literary flights. It is full of rebuttal, it refutes fanciful notions and its closest kin in literature is Thoreau's *Walden*.

In Hudson's view, the experience of Patagonia is a journey to a

OPPOSITE *Granite walls catch first light in cirque of Torres del Paine, Chile.*

higher plane of existence, to a kind of harmony with nature which is the absence of thought; Hudson called this 'animism', the intense love for the visible world.

In the last chapter of Darwin's *Voyage of the Beagle* there is a paragraph which goes as follows:

. . . In calling up images of the past, I find that the plains of Patagonia frequently cross before my eyes; yet these plains are pronounced by all wretched and useless. They can be described only by negative characters; without habitations, without water, without trees, without mountains, they support only a few dwarf plants. Why, then, and the case is not peculiar to myself, have these arid wastes taken so firm a hold of my memory? Why have not the still more level, the greener and more fertile Pampas, which are serviceable to mankind, produced an equal impression? I can scarcely analyse these feelings; but it must be partly owing to the free scope given to the imagination. The plains of Patagonia are boundless, for they are scarcely passable, and hence unknown; they bear the stamp of having thus lasted, as they are now, for ages, and there appears no limit to their duration through future time. If, as the ancients supposed, the flat earth was surrounded by an impassable breadth of water, or by deserts heated to an intolerable excess, who would not look at these last boundaries to man's knowledge with deep but ill-defined sensations?

Hudson understands Darwin's bafflement, but he is not sympathetic to it. Darwin's mistake was that he was looking for something in Patagonia, as in other times people looked for the Andean valley of Trapalanda with its White Indians, or the fabled city of Manoa sought for by Alonzo Pizarro; it is better, Hudson says, to look for nothing at all. Feel it, he says, and be moved by it.

OPPOSITE Native plants on the arid pampa before Macizo del Fitzroy, Argentina.

39

Judging from my own case [Hudson says] I believe that we have here the secret of the persistence of the Patagonian images, and their frequent recurrence in the minds of many who have visited that grey, monotonous, and, in one sense, eminently uninteresting region. It is not the effect of the unknown, it is not imagination; it is that nature in these desolate scenes . . . moves us more deeply than in others.

Later, he becomes specific:

One day while *listening* to the silence, it occurred to my mind to wonder what the effect would be if I were to shout aloud. This seemed at the time a horrible suggestion of fancy, a 'lawless and uncertain thought' which almost made me shudder, and I was anxious to dismiss it quickly from my mind. But during those solitary days it was a rare thing for any thought to cross my mind; animal forms did not cross my vision or bird-voices assail my hearing more rarely. In that novel state of mind I was in, thought had become impossible . . . I had become incapable of reflection: my mind had suddenly transformed itself from a thinking machine into a machine for some other unknown purpose. To think was like setting in motion a noisy engine in my brain; and there was something there which bade me be still, and I was forced to obey. My state was one of *suspense* and *watchfulness*: yet I had no expectation of meeting with an adventure, and felt as free from apprehension as I feel now when sitting in a room in London . . . I was powerless to wonder at or speculate about it; the state seemed familiar rather than strange, and although accompanied by a strong feeling of elation, I did not know it—did not know that something had come between me and my intellect—until I lost it and returned to my former self—to thinking, and the old insipid existence.

OPPOSITE Cuernos del Paine overlooks limestone formations on Lago Nordenskjöld, Chile.

41

Why should this be so in Patagonia, and not in a tropical forest? Well, Hudson says, the tropical forest is full of variety—noise, bird song, colour, animal life: the senses are engaged, but,

. . . in Patagonia the monotony of the plains, or expanse of low hills, the universal unrelieved greyness of everything, and the absence of animal forms and objects new to the eye, leave the mind open and free to receive an impression of nature as a whole. . . . It has a look of antiquity, of desolation, of eternal peace, of a desert that has been a desert from of old and will continue a desert forever; and we know that its only human inhabitants are a few wandering savages—who live by hunting as their progenitors have done for thousands of years.

Emptiness, desolation, the suspension of intellect: Hudson recommended these things when he was miserable in London and remembered the land of lost content. What is Hudson's Patagonia? It is the opposite of a London boarding house.

He had found in Patagonia an American Eden, a peaceable kingdom, where you could see a cow lying down and twenty-six wild pigs using her for a pillow. To be in Patagonia was to surrender to nature and, paradoxically, passion was abolished—none of that fury, only the contentment of the beehive. He speaks with horror of 'books written indoors', of Darwin calling some animals ugly, of the pointlessness of newspapers and the affairs of the world.

How should one die? The perfect death is Patagonian:

The man who finishes his course by a fall from his horse, or is swept away and drowned when fording a swollen stream, has, in most cases, spent a happier life than he who dies of apoplexy in a counting-house or dining-room; or who, finding that end which

OPPOSITE A noble beech tree in the foothills above Río Paine, Chile.

42

seemed so infinitely beautiful to Leigh Hunt (which to me seems so unutterably hateful), drops his white face on the open book before him.

But this, the unutterably hateful way, was how Hudson died.

BRUCE CHATWIN Hudson was wrong in his prediction that Patagonia would remain a desert. The South, at least, turned out to be some of the finest sheep country in the world; and, within thirty years, sheep companies, many of them British, had taken over the territory. The province of Santa Cruz became a country of big houses and shooting parties. My cousin Charley managed to get hold of some of the best land for himself, at Valle Huemeules, within sight of the Cordillera—although he was soon to lose it through the machinations of a 'land-shark who has kindly sworn that my house and all my animals are his'.

While visiting the glacier of Lago Argentino, I called in at the Estancia La Anita, which belongs to the Menendez-Behety family, the sheep-farming moguls of the South. It was here in 1921 that an army of Anarchist revolutionaries, led by a Spanish ex-circus acrobat called Antonio Soto, held hostage about thirty British and other farm managers. When, finally, they surrendered to the Argentine Army, about a hundred and twenty men—nearly all Chileans—were shot into graves they dug themselves, their leaders having nipped away and escaped over the border.

Not all the colonization of Patagonia was like this. Among the immigrants were simple Scottish crofters who had come by way of the Falklands—but the firstcomers, as everyone knows, were the Welsh.

They were refugees from cramped coal-mining valleys and unworkable farms who, just before Hudson's time, went to the Chubut

OPPOSITE Pampa grasses glow in last sunlight at badlands overlooking meanders on Río La Leona, Argentina.

45

River with the intention of founding a New Wales: indeed, there is a case for supposing that modern Welsh nationalism began with the Patagonia colony.

The movement was led by the Revd Michael Jones of Bala, whose agents combed the earth for a stretch of territory unoccupied and uncontaminated by the Union Jack. He had hoped for a mass exodus, but when the time came to leave, there were only a hundred and fifty-three takers—all of whom landed at Puerto Madryn in 1865 off the chartered brig *Mimosa*.

The Welsh are still there. The Eisteddfod is still sung in St David's Hall in Trelew, and around the village of Gaiman there are farms that take you back to the simple agricultural world of Parson Kilvert. It is a little strange for an Englishman to have to speak Spanish to a Mr Jones or a Mr Griffiths. On one farm I met a Mr Williams, whose first cousin, Dr Bryn Williams, came back to Wales, and is now the Archdruid.

By the end of the 1880s the Welsh had outgrown their settlement in the valley; and some of them migrated up river, and carved themselves sheep farms in the foothills of the Cordillera. The village they founded is called Trevelin, the 'Place of the Mill'. The country around it is exactly like parts of Wyoming or Utah; and it's hardly surprising that, when law and order settled in, like a blight, over the American West, some of the more enterprising spirits came down to start a New West in the Absolute South.

One of these characters was a 'defrocked' Texas sheriff called Martin Sheffield, who had a Patagonian career as gold-panner, sharp-shooter and minor crook. In 1922 he announced his discovery of a living dinosaur, a plesiosaurus, in a lake near Epuyen—and made world headlines. (The lake is two and a half feet deep.) Various right-wing newspapers in Buenos Aires found it most flattering to think

OPPOSITE Fitzroy overlooks a bed of stream cobbles deposited along Chorrillo del Salto, Argentina.

46

that Argentina had a Loch Ness Monster of its own—though as a left-wing daily commented: 'This millenarian, pyramidal, apocalyptic animal makes a noise like a madonna and usually appears in the opaline stupors of drunken gringos.'

At the bar in Epuyen, while following up the plesiosaurus story, I talked to some gauchos (this being Patagonia, they were Arab gauchos) whose leader told me that a pair of North American bandits had been living about twenty kilometres along the road at Cholila. I went there next morning and found a perfect specimen of a Western log cabin surrounded by poplars and a corral. The owner said it must have been a beautiful place once and, pointing to the flowered paper coming in shreds off the walls, said: 'Si, señor, there was a film made about those two gentlemen.'

A few months later I was sitting in the State Historical Society of Utah reading this letter, written in the cabin and dated 10 August 1902:

My dear friend,

I suppose you have thought long before that I had forgotten you (or was dead) but, my dear friend, I am still alive, and when I think of my old friends you are always the first to come to mind. It will probably surprise you to hear from me away down in this country but U.S. was too small for me the last two years I was there. I was restless. I wanted to see more of the world. I had seen all of the U.S. that I thought was good . . . another of my uncles died and left $30,000 to our little family of 3 so I took my $10,000 and started to see a little more of the world. I visited the best cities and the best parts of South A. till I got here. And this part of the country looked so good that I located, and I think for good, for I like the

place better every day. I have 300 cattle, 1,500 sheep, and 28 good saddle horses, 2 men to do my work, also a good 4 room house, warehouse, stable, chicken house and some chickens. The only thing lacking is a cook, for I am living in single cussidness [*sic*] and sometimes I feel very lonely for I am alone all day, and my neighbours don't amount to anything, besides the only language spoken in this country is Spanish, and I don't speak it well enough to converse on the latest scandals so dear to the hearts of all nations. . . .

The writer was an ex-Mormon called Robert Leroy Parker, better known as Butch Cassidy, at that time the most wanted outlaw in the United States, with a string of perfectly executed bank and train robberies behind him. The recipient of the letter, back in Utah, was a Mrs Davies, mother-in-law of Cassidy's greatest friend, Elza Lay. The 'little family of 3' was a *ménage à trois* consisting of Cassidy, Harry Longabaugh—the 'Sundance Kid'—and the Kid's wife, a beautiful schoolteacher from Denver called Etta Place—who may or may not have been the granddaughter of the 5th Earl of Essex. The 'dead uncle' who gave them the $30,000 was the Wild Bunch Gang's robbery on the First National Bank of Winnemucca, Nevada, on 10 September 1900.

This was their last hold-up in the United States. Already the pace had got too hot for them when the Union Pacific Railroad put mounted rangers in their box cars. The purpose of the robbery was to get enough money to set sail for South America. After it was over, the disbanded Wild Bunch Gang rode to Fort Worth; had their farewell photograph taken, and sent a copy to the bank manager in Winnemucca, in whose office it still hangs.

The 'little family of 3' then went to New York, where the Kid bought Etta a gold watch at Tiffany's; and they both had their pho-

OPPOSITE Moonrise over Lago Sarmiento at dusk, Chile.

51

tograph taken again. They also went to the Metropolitan Opera where the Kid, whose real name was Leinbach, is said to have become a devoted Wagnerian. They sailed to Buenos Aires, won a concession of land at Cholila, and settled there. Three years later, possibly to finance a trip to Europe (one outlaw historian claims they went to the Bayreuth Festival), they staged a bank robbery in Río Gallegos, the Argentine port near the Straits of Magellan. On returning from Europe, they settled again in Cholila, but soon afterwards, with the help of the New York photograph, they were traced there by the Pinkerton Agency. They sold the cabin and left in a hurry, for Bolivia, where they are supposed to have died in a shootout with the Army—at least, this is the version you see in the movie.

But I must warn anyone who is tempted to take up outlaw history that it is a most dementing subject, in that your characters can have up to ten aliases and die in ten different places. The Pinkerton Agency has three different deaths for Butch Cassidy on its files, none of them in Bolivia. For myself, I would like to think that Cassidy and his gang returned from Bolivia in 1909; that, in a fracas with the Argentine Frontier Police, the Kid was killed in 1910; and that Cassidy himself went back to the United States and died in his bed. In 1925 he is supposed to have revisited his old horse-dealer at Sheep Creek Canyon, Utah; and to have stayed again in the cabin where, between train robberies, he would hole up and read the works of Lord Macaulay. He is also supposed to have eaten blueberry pie with his old father in the family house at Circleville: at least that is what his sister told me, Lula Parker Betenson, still very much alive at the age of ninety-four.

OPPOSITE Grasses punctuate a boggy area in a beech forest in the Cordillera de los Andes, Chile.

52

PAUL THEROUX   The first sighting of a giant was reported by Antonio Pigafetta who kept a journal during the three years (1519–22) when

he sailed with Magellan on the first voyage round the world. It was round about September 1521 near San Julian:

> . . . One day, without anyone expecting it, we saw a giant, who was on the shore of the sea, quite naked, and was dancing and leaping, and singing, and whilst singing he put the sand and dust on his head. Our captain sent one of his men towards him, whom he charged to sing and leap like the other to reassure him, and show him friendship. This he did, and immediately the sailor led this giant to a little island where the captain was waiting for him; and when he was before us he began to be astonished, and to be afraid, and he raised one finger on high, thinking that we came from heaven. He was so tall that the tallest of us only came up to his waist. . . .

The giant's face was painted red and yellow, with two hearts painted on his cheeks, and his nearly hairless head was painted white. He wore well-sewn clothes of skins and thick fur boots on his feet. Shown his image in a mirror, he was terrified and enraged.

> . . . The captain named this kind of people Pataghom [on account of their large feet]* who have no houses, but have huts made of the skins of the animals with which they clothe themselves, and go hither and thither with these huts of theirs, as the gypsies do; they live on raw meat, and eat a certain sweet root, which they call Capac. These two giants that we had in the ship ate a large basketful of biscuit, and rats without skinning them, and they drank half a bucket of water at each time.

Magellan decided to kidnap two giants as a present for Charles V and his Queen Empress. The two giants had been tricked into being

OPPOSITE Grasses along Río Paine in evening shadows of Torres del Paine, Chile.

*An editorial interpolation in the 1874 edition.

55

manacled, but when they saw they were caught they puffed and blew and they foamed 'like bulls, crying out very loud "Setebos", that is to say, the great devil, that he should help them'. There was a great fuss, and a fight, but in time both giants were baptized. Though the idea was to bring the Big-Feet back to Spain, the giants died—the one baptized Paulo in the Pacific—and only Pigafetta's written account was to return.

Shakespeare read the account. The evidence is in *The Tempest*. Compare

> . . . he raised one finger on high, thinking that we came from heaven

with

> *Caliban:* Hast thou not dropped from heaven?
> *Stephano:* Out o' the moon, I do assure thee: I was the man in the moon, when time was.

Compare

> . . . crying out . . . 'Setebos', . . . the great devil

with

> *Caliban:* I must obey: his art is of such power
> It would control my dam's god, Setebos,
> And make a vassal of him.

The giants were described by other early explorers: de Weert, Spelbergen and Shelvocke, and they adopted Magellan's term, *Patagones*, 'big feet'. Byron's grandfather met the Big-Feet and in a curious picture he is shown watching a giant Patagonian woman rather anxiously—he comes up to her midriff. How he happened to be

OPPOSITE Upper Salto Grande cascades below Cuernos del Paine and morning clouds, Chile.

56

in Patagonia is a long story, of shipwreck and starvation and heroic survival, which Peter Shankland tells in *Byron of the Wager*. Shankland writes:

> Thomas Cavendish had measured the imprint of one of their feet and found it to be eighteen inches long. Byron on tip-toes could just reach the top of the head of one of the Patagonians.
>
> Their middle stature seemed to be about eight feet; 'their extreme, nine and upwards', one of his officers wrote. The giants, with time, seemed to be getting more gigantic; their feet, in successive reports, even bigger.

'Patagons' are mentioned by Thomas Falkner in his *A Description of Patagonia* (1774). Falkner arrived in Argentina quite by chance in 1731. He was unwell, but was looked after by some Irish Jesuits and in time became a convert to the Catholic faith, and travelled throughout Patagonia as a missionary. Falkner said that the Tehuelches are known in Europe 'by the name of Patagons' and though he attests to their great size, he describes the human bones he has found as even more enormous:

> On the banks of the River Carcarania, or Tercero, about three or four leagues before it enters into the Parana, are found great numbers of bones, of an extraordinary bigness, which seem human. There are some greater and some less, as if they were of persons of different ages. I have seen thigh-bones, ribs, breast-bones, and pieces of skulls. I have also seen teeth, and particularly some grinders which were three inches in diameter at the base. These bones (as I have been informed) are likewise found on the banks of the Rivers Parana and Paraguay. . . . The Indian historian, Gar-

OPPOSITE Firebrush blooms in foothills above Río Serrano, Chile.

59

cilasso de la Vega Inga, makes mention of these bones in Peru, and tells us that the Indians have a tradition, that giants formerly inhabited those countries, and were destroyed by God for the crime of sodomy.

This book was studied by Darwin and was in the library of the *Beagle* (Darwin refers to the author as 'Falconer'). Darwin, in consequence, was on the lookout for the giants. In Cape Gregory, he writes,

> We had an interview . . . with the famous so-called gigantic Patagonians, who gave us a cordial reception. Their height appears greater than it really is, from their large guanaco mantles, their long flowing hair, and general figure: on an average their height is about six feet, with some men taller and only a few shorter; and the women are also tall; altogether they are certainly the tallest race which we anywhere saw.

Their faces were painted; they spoke a little English and Spanish because they had had contact with sealers and whalers. He found them half-civilized and 'proportionally demoralized'.

Fifty years later, Lady Florence Dixie set sail for Patagonia ('Land of the Giants') 'because it was an outlandish place and so far away'. With her were Lord Queensberry, Lord James Douglas, her husband and brothers.

> We only took one servant with us, knowing that English servants inevitably prove a nuisance and hindrance in expeditions of the kind, when a great deal of 'roughing it' has to be gone through, as they have an unpleasant knack of falling ill at inopportune moments.

ABOVE Weathered beech trunk in the Cordillera de los Andes, Argentina.

OPPOSITE Chorrillo del Salto cascades in evening shadows of Cerro Fitzroy, Argentina.

60

After some months of travel they found themselves (at Punta Arenas) in the presence of a real Patagonian Indian. They thought him a 'singularly unprepossessing object, and, for the sake of his race, we hoped an unfavourable specimen of it'. He was dirty, but Lady Florence was further disappointed by his size and the size of his fellow tribesmen:

> I was not struck so much by their height as by their extraordinary development of chest and muscle. As regards their stature, I do not think the average height of the men exceeded six feet, and as my husband stands six feet two inches I had a favourable opportunity for forming an accurate estimate. One or two there were, certainly, who towered far above him, but these were exceptions.

In one respect, Lady Florence was satisfied: on the Indians' feet were boots, large, and appropriately Patagonian.

In *The Tempest*, Caliban seems to stand for 'the betrayed native'. In Pigafetta and in Falkner, the Indians are large and handsome and numerous. Darwin reports them as not so numerous, not very big, and rather miserable and abject. They have been visited by Europe, and diminished by it. Lady Florence Dixie sees them as 'fast approaching extinction' and smaller than her husband and, she says, 'numbering no more than 800 souls'. Fifty years later, the Patagonian giants—or rather one small Patagonian Indian—were gone.

BRUCE CHATWIN And yet Patagonia cannot, and never could have meant Big-Foot. 'Pata' is indeed a 'foot' or 'hoof' in Spanish but the suffix '-gon' is meaningless. Even Drake's chaplain, Francis Fletcher, knew there was something wrong and tried to turn the Patagonians into 'Pentagours'—meaning 'five cubits high', which would bring them to seven and a half feet. And then my attention was

OPPOSITE Powerful *williwaws* blow clouds of water spray across Lago Nordenskjöld, Chile.

62

drawn to a late medieval romance called *Primaleon of Greece*, in which a strange beast called Patagon appears.

The book was written by an unknown author and published in Spain in 1512, that is, seven years before Magellan sailed. It was translated by Shakespeare's friend Anthony Mundy in 1596, fifteen years before *The Tempest*. I believe that both Magellan and Shakespeare read it.

Primaleon of Greece is one of those interminable sagas which, in the sixteenth century, were considered extremely exciting. It runs to about 800 packed pages, and was the kind of book an explorer might take on a long journey as we might take away Proust. The most famous example of the genre was the *Book of Amadis*.

In the first book of *Primaleon*, the hero dashes around Europe, rescues damsels in distress, fights giants, helps the Emperor of Constantinople against the Turks, makes friends with Prince Edward of England, and does all the respectable things a knight should do. Then, at the end of Book II, he sails to a faraway island, where the King's son, a boy called Prince Palantine, tells him of a people who live in the hinterland—absolute savages who eat raw flesh and wear the skins of beasts:

> But this is nothing, in regard of one of them, which most usually is seene, and whom we call Patagon, said to be engendred by a Beast in the woods, being the strangest misshapen and counterfeite creature in the world. He hath good understanding, is amorous of women, and keepeth company with one of whom (it is said) he was engendred. . . .

In other words, Patagon is a latter-day equivalent of Grendel.

He hath the face of a Dogge, great eares, which hang down upon

OPPOSITE A hearty beech tree growing in limestone frames Glaciar Grey and Campo de Hielo Sur, Chile.

his shoulders, his teeth sharpe and big, standing out of his mouth very much: his feete are like a Hart's, and he runneth wondrous lightly. Such as have seene him tell mervallous matters of him, because he chaseth ordinarily among the mountaines with two Lyons in a chaine like a lease, and a bow in his hand. . . .

The moment the Knight hears of Patagon, he decides to go out hunting; and, after a tremendous struggle, fells him with two sound strokes of his sword:

> Now through the grievous paine he [Patagon] felt by his wounds, as also his losse of blood, which dyed the grasse round about him, he was no longer able to stand on his legs, but falling on the earth, roared so dreadfully, as it would have terrified the very stoutest heart. . . .

With a right and a left, the Knight then gets rid of the two lions; trusses Patagon up with their leashes, and ships him aboard as a present for Queen Gridonia of Polonia, because, secretly, he is in love with her daughter, the Princess Zephira. On the journey the Patagon behaves quite dreadfully, but finally they reach port, where the Queen is persuaded to go on board ship. She takes one look at the monster and says: 'This can be nothing else but a divel . . . hee gets no cherishing at my hands.'

The Princess Zephira, however, is a far more spirited girl than her mother. She takes an immediate fancy to the Beast and advances

> . . . boldly to Patagon, bidding him go along with her, stroking his head and using him very kindely: which made him forget his former stubbornesse, and fall at her feete, for he greatly delighted to gaze faire ladies in the face, so taking his chaine in her hand, he followed after her as gently, as if he had beene a Spaniell. . . .

66

We should perhaps explain here that the 'Giant' Tehuelche Indians were reported, as early as the sixteenth century, to have worn dog-headed 'vizzards' or masks—which is why Magellan would have said, 'Ha! Patagon!' when he saw one of these creatures dancing on the shore at St Julian. It will also explain why, in *The Tempest*, the comic Stephano says of Caliban, 'I shall laugh myself to death at this puppy-headed monster.'

I think we have here a situation in which a bad novel inspired a great explorer to do something shoddy, which, in turn, inspired the greatest playwright to one of his greatest creations.

PAUL THEROUX The Fuegian Indians confirmed Darwin's ideas about the origins of our species and his suspicions that some men had evolved further than others. It was the Indian as a fisherman and a canoe-maker that interested him and other travellers to Patagonia. These are the key texts.

[Pigafetta] . . . In this place they have boats, which are made of a tree, all in one piece, which they call 'canoo'. These are not made with iron instruments, for they have not got any, but with stones, like pebbles, and with these they plane and dig out these boats. Into these thirty or forty men enter, and their oars are made like iron shovels; and those who row these oars are black people, quite naked and shaven, and look like enemies of hell. . . .

[Francis Fletcher] This cannowe, or boate, was made of the barke of divers trees, having a prowe and a sterne standing up, and semicirclewise yeelding inward, of one form and fashion, the body whereof was a most dainty mould, bearing in it most comely proportion and excellent workmanship, in so much as to our Generall

OPPOSITE Sandstone totem pole formations reach toward afternoon clouds drifting above the pampa, Argentina.

and us, it seemed never to have beene done without the cunning and expert judgement of art; and that not for the use of so rude and barbarous a people, but for the pleasure of some great and noble personage, yea, of some Prince. It had no other closing up or caulking in the seames, but the stitching with thongs made of seal skins, or other such beast, and yet so close that it received very little or no water at all.

[Falkner] These Indians live near the sea, on both sides of the straits. . . . They are sometimes attacked by the Huilliches, and the other Tehuelhets, who carry them away for slaves, as they have nothing to lose but their liberty and their lives. They live chiefly on fish: which they catch, either by diving, or striking them with their darts. They are very nimble of foot, and catch guanacoes and ostriches with their bowls [bolas]. Their stature is much the same as that of the other Tehuelhets, rarely exceeding seven feet, and oftentimes not six feet. They are an innocent, harmless people.

[Darwin] December 17th, 1832. . . . When we came within hail, one of the four natives who were present advanced to receive us, and began to shout most vehemently, wishing to direct us where to land. When we were on shore the party looked rather alarmed, but continued talking and making gestures with great rapidity. It was without exception the most curious and interesting spectacle I ever beheld: I could not have believed how wide was the difference between savage and civilised man; it is greater than between a wild and domesticated animal, inasmuch as in man there is a greater power of improvement. . . .
December 25th. . . . While going one day on shore near Wollaston Island, we pulled alongside a canoe with six Fuegians. These

OPPOSITE Ancient hand paintings on a sandstone wall on the pampa, Argentina.

70

were the most abject and miserable creatures I anywhere beheld . . . [they] were quite naked, and even one full-grown woman was absolutely so. It was raining heavily, and the fresh water, together with the spray, trickled down her body. In another harbour not far distant, a woman, who was suckling a recently-born child, came one day alongside the vessel, and remained there out of mere curiosity, whilst the sleet fell and thawed on her naked bosom, and on the skin of her naked baby! These poor wretches were stunted in their growth, their hideous faces bedaubed with white paint, their skins filthy and greasy, their hair entangled, their voices discordant, and their gestures violent. Viewing such men, one can hardly make oneself believe that they are fellow-creatures, and inhabitants of the same world. . . .

Their country is a broken mass of wild rocks, lofty hills, and useless forests; and these are viewed through mists and endless storms. The habitable land is reduced to the stones on the beach; in search of food they are compelled unceasingly to wander from spot to spot, and so steep is the coast that they can only move about in their wretched canoes. They cannot know the feeling of having a home, and still less that of domestic affection; for the husband is to the wife a brutal master to a laborious slave. . . . Their skill in some respects may be compared to the instinct of animals; for it is not improved by experience: the canoe, their most ingenious work, poor as it is, has remained the same, as we know from Drake, for the last two hundred and fifty years. . . .

BRUCE CHATWIN One of the books that Darwin took aboard the *Beagle* was Captain James Weddell's *Voyage towards the South Pole* (in the brig *Jane* and the cutter *Beaufoy*). Weddell sailed further south than anyone had yet ventured, and on 8 February 1822, at latitude

ABOVE Oligocene-age clay hills on the pampa at sunset, Argentina.

OPPOSITE Rounded rocks and tidal basins below bluffs at Punta Norte at sunrise on the Atlantic coast, Argentina.

73

74° 15′ he saw whales, 'birds of the blue petrel kind', and leagues of open sea. He wrote on his chart: 'Sea of George IV—Navigable', and left the impression that the sea became warmer as one neared the Pole.

Returning northwards to the Cape Horn Archipelago, at Hermit Island he ran in with canoeloads of Fuegians who threatened to over-run the ship. He managed to persuade them to sit still while he read a chapter of the Bible—to which they listened with solemn faces, one man believing that the book itself talked.

Weddell then jotted down some words of their language and concluded that it was Hebrew, though how it had travelled to Cape Horn was, he admitted, 'a question of interest to philologists'.

Now it happened that, while Darwin was writing his *Journal* during the voyage of the *Beagle*, a copy of Captain Weddell's book lay on the desk of the editor of the *Southern Literary Messenger* in Richmond, Virginia—Edgar Allen Poe.

Poe himself was a solitary wanderer, obsessed by voyages of annihilation and rebirth; and he used Weddell's *Voyage towards the South Pole* to help him write his novel of a crazed, self-destructive journey. In *The Narrative of Arthur Gordon Pym*, the narrator lands on a warm Antarctic island called Tsalal where everything is black, including the bestial savages who swarm aboard the ship called *Jane*. Their language, too, is a variety of Hebrew—in other words, the Tsalalians are Fuegians transformed into fiction, with a smattering of Poe's own anti-Negro prejudices thrown in.

Pym is one of the nastiest, most brilliant and, in its effect on the imagination, influential books of the nineteenth century. It inspired Dostoevsky to write one of his rare literary essays; and because Baudelaire was its translator into French, it inspired a whole series of 'voyage' poems—from Baudelaire's own incomparable 'Le Voyage'

OPPOSITE Glaciar Moreno at daybreak during a clearing rainstorm, Argentina.

('Mais les vrais voyageurs sont ceux-là qui partent seulement pour partir . . .') to Rimbaud's prose poem 'Being Beauteous'.

But the Fuegians themselves, who helped to set all this off, were a rather gentle people, who lived according to the rhythm of the seasons, and were contented with their lot. Towards the end of the last century, the Revd Thomas Bridges settled on the Beagle Channel as a missionary; and before his Indians died out, from epidemics, he managed to compile a dictionary of their language. This dictionary is now their monument. It would perhaps have surprised Darwin to learn that a young man of the Yaghan tribe had a vocabulary of around 30,000 words, perhaps even more than Shakespeare ever wrote. If anyone has time to spare, I do recommend them to take a look at Bridges's original manuscript in the British Museum: for the images that surface from its pages of crabbed handwriting are often of unimaginable beauty.

PAUL THEROUX Nor is it fair to judge the Indians from that most memorable passage in Captain Joshua Slocum's *Sailing Alone around the World* (1900):

> . . . the natives, Patagonian and Fuegian . . . were as squalid as contact with unscrupulous traders could make them. A large percentage of the business there [in Punta Arenas] was traffic in 'fire-water'. If there was a law against selling the poisonous stuff to the natives, it was not enforced. Fine specimens of the Patagonian race, looking smart in the morning when they came into town, had repented before night of ever having seen a white man, so beastly drunk were they, to say nothing about the peltry of which they had been robbed. . . . Just previous to my arrival the governor, himself of a jovial turn of mind, had sent a party of young bloods to

OPPOSITE Lichens cover a large basalt boulder in badlands on the pampa, Argentina.

77

foray a Fuegian settlement and wipe out what they could of it on account of the recent massacre of a schooner's crew somewhere else. . . . The port captain, a Chilean naval officer, advised me to ship hands to fight Indians in the strait farther west, and spoke of my stopping until a gunboat should be going through, which would give me a tow. I said no more about the matter, but simply loaded my guns. At this point in my dilemma Captain Pedro Samblich, a good Austrian of large experience, coming along, gave me a bag of carpet-tacks, worth more than all the fighting men and dogs of Tierra del Fuego. I protested that I had no use for carpet-tacks on board. Samblich smiled at my want of experience, and maintained stoutly that I would have use for them. 'You must use them with discretion,' he said; 'that is to say, don't step on them yourself.' With this remote hint about the use of the tacks I got on all right, and saw the way to maintain clear decks at night without the care of watching. . . .

Soon he is in the middle of the Strait, passing Thieves' Bay, 'suggestively named':

. . . As drowsiness came on I sprinkled the deck with tacks, and then I turned in, bearing in mind the advice of my old friend Samblich that I was not to step on them myself. I saw to it that not a few of them stood 'business end' up; for when the *Spray* passed Thieves' Bay two canoes had put out and followed in her wake, and there was no disguising the fact any longer that I was alone.

Now, it is well-known that one cannot step on a tack without saying something about it. A pretty good Christian will whistle when he steps on the 'commercial-end' of a carpet tack; a savage will howl and claw the air, and that was just what happened that night about twelve o'clock, while I was alseep in the cabin, where

the savages thought they 'had me', sloop and all, but changed their minds when they stepped on deck, for then they thought that I or someone else had them. I had no need of a dog; they howled like a pack of hounds. I had hardly use for a gun. They jumped pell-mell, some into their canoes and some into the sea, to cool off, I suppose, and there was a deal of free language over it as they went. I fired several guns when I came on deck, to let the rascals know that I was home, and then I turned in again, feeling sure I should not be disturbed any more by people who left in so great a hurry.

The Fuegians, being cruel, are naturally cowards. . . .

And then there were none. . . . The extinction of the Yaghan, a rough parallel of what happened to all the Fuegian tribes, is recorded as follows:

Date		Yaghan
1834	The year the *Beagle* left Tierra del Fuego Then came the sealers and the whalers	3,000
1880	Missionaries counted 7,000 to 8,000 among all the tribes. There would be	1,200
1888	Barclay's estimate	800
1889	Argentine Government distributed clothes to the shivering, half-starved Yaghan, and counted	400
1908	Barclay counted again	170
1924	Lothrop's figures	50

OPPOSITE Talus blocks and glacial cirque below Torres del Paine, Chile.

81

ABOVE Figworts bloom in vernal patterns
on the pampa, Argentina.

OPPOSITE Wind-formed beech tree grows
above whitewater in a gorge on Río
Paine, Chile.

Lothrop wrote in 1925:

Later in the same year [1925] an epidemic of measles ravaged Tierra del Fuego. What happened to the Yaghan I do not know, but Mr William Bridges wrote me that more than twenty adult Ona and an unknown number of children had died. With the exception of a few mixed bloods the Indians of Tierra del Fuego are probably extinct.

All that is left of them is a monument in the little plaza of Ushuaia, 'al Indio'.

BRUCE CHATWIN Tierra del Fuego is, of course, 'The Land of Fire'; and the most usual explanation of its origin is that Magellan saw the camp fires of the Indians and called it 'Fireland'. Someone else has suggested that there were active volcanoes at the time; but this is not, geologically, correct. Another version says that Magellan saw the smoke of the camp fires only; called it Tierra del Humo; but that the Emperor Charles V, seeing that name on a map, said there was no smoke without fire, and changed it.

The evidence for the first explanation comes from Maximilian Transylvanicus, the man who interviewed the survivors on their return to Spain:

The month of November was upon them, the night was rather more than five hours long, and they had never seen any human beings on the shore. But one night a great number of fires were seen, mostly on their left hand, from which they guessed that they had been seen by the natives of the region. But Magellan, seeing that the country was rocky and also stark with eternal cold, thought it useless to waste many days in examining it.

Magellan was wise to move on; for the weather in the Strait is usually infernal. In fact, he was so exceptionally lucky that when he sailed out into what is usually one of the most violent seas in the world, he chanced on a flat calm, and called it the Pacific.

There is, however, another dimension to the Fireland problem. Cape Horn was rounded for the first time in 1619 by two Dutchmen, Schouten and Le Maire, who named the headland, not after its shape, or the shape of South America, but for their home port, Hoorn, in Holland. Before that, Tierra del Fuego was thought to be the tip of the Unknown Antarctic Continent, the Antichthon or Anti-Earth, whose existence was originally postulated by Pythagoras. The Antichthon was an upside-down country, absolutely not meant for human beings, where snow fell upwards, trees grew downwards, the sun shone black, and its inhabitants were the sixteen-fingered Antipodeans who danced themselves into ecstasy. 'We cannot go to them,' it was said. 'They cannot come to us.' It was, in other words, some kind of Hell. Small wonder, then, that Magellan refused to land.

For, from the moment America had been discovered, from the moment that the discoveries of Columbus and Vespucci were recorded by the cartographers of Europe, it was obvious that a Strait of Water had to separate this Dreadful Place from the rest of creation. One map-maker, Martin of Bohemia, accordingly took the obvious step of drawing in the Strait, which Magellan proceeded to discover.

The issue was further complicated by certain medieval notions about the Other Side of the Globe. Dante, for example, believed with the Greeks that the entire Southern Hemisphere was uninhabited, uninhabitable and thus out of bounds for man. One of the most arresting passages in the *Inferno* relates the southern voyage of Ulysses in search of the Mountain of Purgatory, which lay at the heart of the Antichthon, and from which no man returned. Dante takes as his

OPPOSITE Clouds at dawn over Valle Frances in Cordillera Paine, Chile.

85

starting point the lines of the *Odyssey* where the blind prophet, Tiresias, predicts that the hero will not be content to sit at home with Penelope in Ithaca, but that death will come to him from out of the sea. In Canto 26, Dante and Virgil find Ulysses burning in the Eighth Ring of Hell for having attempted to reach the forbidden mountain, not as a dead soul, but as a living man thirsting for knowledge.

Here, in one of the greatest of all passages that describe the explorer's passion to get to the back of beyond, is Ulysses' own account of how he persuaded his men to follow him out of the Mediterranean, and through the Pillars of Hercules:

'O brothers,' I said, 'who through a hundred thousand dangers have reached the west, to this so brief vigil of our senses that remains to us, choose not to deny experience, following the sun, of the world that has no people. Consider your origin: you were not made to live as brutes, but to pursue virtue and knowledge.'

With this little speech I made my companions so keen for the voyage that then I could hardly have held them back. And turning our stern to the morning, we made of our oars wings for the mad flight, always gaining on the left. The night now saw the other pole and all its stars, and ours so low that it did not rise from the ocean floor. Five times the light beneath the moon had been rekindled and as many quenched, since we had entered on the passage of the deep, when there appeared to us a mountain dark in the distance, and to me it seemed the highest I had ever seen. We rejoiced, but soon our joy was turned to grief, for from the new land a whirlwind rose and struck the forepart of the ship. Three times it whirled her round with all the waters, and the fourth time it lifted the stern aloft and plunged the prow below, as pleased Another, till the sea closed over us.

OPPOSITE Summer snow accents lower ramparts of Paine Grande, Chile.

86

And this, of course, is the passage that gave Tennyson the idea for his own 'Ulysses':

> It little profits that an idle king,
> By this still hearth, among these barren crags,
> Matched with an agèd wife, I mete and dole,
> Unequal laws unto a savage race,
> That hoard, and sleep, and feed, and know not me.
> I cannot rest from travel: I will drink
> Life to the lees . . .

PAUL THEROUX Canto 26 also gave Poe the end to *The Narrative of Arthur Gordon Pym*; for when the hero finally escapes from the island of Tsalal in a canoe, he plunges on southwards into a vortex of destruction:

March 22. The darkness had materially increased, relieved only by the glare of the water thrown back from the white curtain before us. Many gigantic and pallidly white birds flew continuously now from beyond the veil, and their scream was the eternal *Tekeli-li!* as they retreated from our vision. Hereupon Nu-Nu stirred in the bottom of the boat; but upon touching him, we found his spirit departed. And now we rushed into the embraces of the cataract, where a chasm threw itself open to receive us. But there arose in our pathway a shrouded human figure, very far larger in its proportions than any dweller among men. And the hue of the skin of the figure was of the perfect whiteness of the snow.

And here, in yet another variant, is the sinking of the *Pequod* from *Moby Dick*:

OPPOSITE Summer snow dusts Paine Grande above icebergs in Lago Grey, Chile.

89

For an instant, the tranced boat's crew stood still; then turned. 'The ship? Great God, where is the ship?' Soon they through dim, bewildering mediums saw her sidelong fading phantom, as in the gaseous Fata Morgana; only the uppermost masts out of water; while fixed by infatuation, or fidelity, or fate, to their once lofty perches, the pagan harpooners still maintained their sinking look-outs on the sea. And now, concentric circles seized the lone boat it-self, and all its crew, and each floating oar, and every lance-pole, and spinning, animate and inanimate, all round and round in one vortex, carried the smallest chip of the *Pequod* out of sight.

BRUCE CHATWIN To return to Dante: in the second book of the *Divine Comedy*, the 'Purgatorio', Dante and Virgil emerge from Hell; travel across a solitary plain; see from afar 'the trembling of the sea', and finally come to a desert shore 'that never saw any man navigate its waters who afterwards had experience of return'. Standing at the water's edge, they meet the souls of the dead who await the Boatman to ferry them across the water to the Mountain of Purgatory: the summit they can see in the distance. Dante, too, waits his turn; but, unlike Ulysses, he has been fortunate enough to pluck the Golden Bough—which is his passport to return to the land of the living.

Now when the truth of Magellan's discoveries began to filter through Europe, the poets, at least, saw him as a new Ulysses. And even Magellan himself, as he careered on his south-westerly course down the coast of Patagonia, must have been reminded of the arche-typal mariner's 'mad track' to the bottom of the globe. The mutinies he had to suppress testify to the terror of his men; and when they peered across the Strait at the north shore of Fireland, they could per-haps be forgiven for mistaking the Fuegian camp fires for dead souls burning in Hell.

OPPOSITE Double rainbow over Laguna Armaga and Cordillera Paine, Chile.

90

Certainly, the poets of Renaissance Europe were soon busy weaving mythologies out of Magellan, of Ulysses, of Straits, of Ferrymen, Death and Resurrection. One was the Andalucian Don Luis de Góngora, who, in his *First Solitude*, describes Magellan's Strait as 'the elusive hinge of silver':

> Hinge that unites, one ocean, the two seas,
> Whether the carpet of the morning star
> It kisses, or the rocks of Hercules.

But no one has ever described the 'south-west passage' to the next life more wonderfully than John Donne on his deathbed:

> Since I am comming to that Holy roome,
>   Where, with thy Quire of Saints for evermore,
> I shall be made thy Musique; As I come
>   I tune the Instrument here at the dore,
>   And what I must doe then, thinke here before.
>
> Whilst my Physitians by their love are growne
>   Cosmographers, and I their Mapp, who lie
> Flat on this bed, that by them may be showne
>   That this is my South-west discoverie
>   *Per fretum febris*, by these streights to die,
>
> I joy, that in these straits, I see my West;
>   For, though theire currants yeeld returne to none,
> What shall my West hurt me? As West and East
>   In all flatt Maps (and I am one) are one,
>   So death doth touch the Resurrection.

OPPOSITE Fringed with salt nodules, the waters of Laguna Armaga reflect Cordillera Paine, Chile.

93

Is the Pacifique Sea my home? Or are
   The Easterne riches? Is *Jerusalem*?
Anyan, and *Magellan*, and *Gibraltare*,
   All streights, and none but streights, are wayes to them,
   Whether where *Japhet* dwelt, or *Cham*, or *Sem*.

We thinke that *Paradise* and *Calvarie*,
   Christs Crosse, and *Adams* tree, stood in one place;
Looke Lord, and finde both *Adams* met in me;
   As the first *Adams* sweat surrounds my face,
   May the last *Adams* blood my soule embrace.

So, in his purple wrapp'd receive mee Lord,
   By these his thornes give me his other Crowne;
And as to others soules I preach'd thy word,
   Be this my Text, my Sermon to mine owne,
   Therfore that he may raise the Lord throws down.

Imagine my delight then to find that the legend of the Boatman survives quite independently among the Indians in this part of the world. My last days in the South were spent on the soft green island of Chiloe, which traditionally sends its young men as migrant workers to the sheep ranches of Patagonia. The island is all but divided by two lakes, Huillinco and Cucao, which flow out into the Pacific, and along which the souls of the dead are thought to be ferried before crossing the sea to the other world.

I found the road to Cucao as bad as it had been in Darwin's day: so, like him a hundred and forty years before, I decided to take the ferry. Had he, however, known the legend of the Ferryman, I doubt he'd have risked this note in his diary:

The periagua was a strange rough boat, but the crew were even stranger. I doubt if six uglier little men ever got into a boat together.

Cucao, when I got there, reminded me of those reconstructions of Norse settlements you sometimes see in Scandinavian museums. In the largest house I was offered a bed and, that evening, by the fireside, I met an old Indian story-teller called Don Antonio. He told of Millalobo, a kind of merman who'd made off with one of the neighbour's daughters and taken her to live in a palace at the bottom of the lagoon. He told of sea-monsters, the Basilisk, the Thrauco, the Sirens and the Pincoya, a red-haired sea-nymph who encouraged the shellfish to multiply.

In the last of the light, he pointed to a black rock at the end of the bay and said it was the Boatman's landing-stage.

'Once,' he said, 'I knew a man who laughed at the story of the Boatman. We warned him; but he went out there, and stood on the rock, and shouted, "Boatman! Boatman!"—and the Boatman came.'

SOURCES

The Poems of Samuel Taylor Coleridge, edited by Ernest Hartley Coleridge, London, 1931.

Dante Alighieri, *The Divine Comedy*, translated by Charles S. Singleton, London, 1971–5.

Darwin, Charles, *Journal of Researches into the Natural History and Geology of the Countries Visited during the Voyage round the World of H.M.S. Beagle . . .* London, 1902.

Dixie, Lady Florence, *Across Patagonia*, London, 1880.

The Poems of John Donne, edited by Sir Herbert Grierson, Oxford, 1933.

The World Encompassed by Sir Francis Drake . . . Carefully Collected out of the Notes of Master Francis Fletcher, London, 1628.

Falkner, Thomas, *A Description of Patagonia*, Hereford, 1774.

Góngora y Argote, Luis de, *The Solitudes*, translated by Edward Meryon Wilson, Cambridge, 1965.

Hudson, W. H., *Idle Days in Patagonia*, London, 1893.

Lothrop, Samuel Kirkland, *The Indians of Tierra del Fuego*, New York, 1928.

OPPOSITE Fitzroy looms above forested ridges behind Laguna Capri, Argentina.

97

The First Voyage round the World, by Magellan, translated from the accounts of Pigafetta, and other contemporary writers, edited by Lord Stanley of Alderley, Hakluyt Society, vol. LII, London, 1874.

Melville, Herman, *Moby Dick*, London, 1946.

Poe, Edgar Allan, *The Narrative of Arthur Gordon Pym*, New York, 1960.

The Famous and Renowned Historie of Primaleon of Greece, translated by A[nthony] M[unday], London, 1619.

Shankland, Peter, *Captain Byron of the Wager*, London, 1975.

Shelvocke, George, *A Voyage round the World*, London, 1726.

Slocum (Joshua), *Sailing Alone around the World*, London, 1900.

The Poems of Tennyson, edited by Christopher Ricks, London, 1969.

OPPOSITE Petrified logs and wood chips lie in ancient piles on the pampa, Argentina.

NOTES ON THE PHOTOGRAPHS

GIFFORD HICKEY introduced me to Patagonia. He sent thick envelopes of material and stories about his travels and adventures there. As I read I realized the deep respect he has for this little-known land. Canoeing down Río Baker, sailing off Isla Gajtecas, climbing in Cordillera Paine, floating Río Santa Cruz, paddling on Canal Beagle—in ten years of travel he had experienced a Patagonia few other people have ever seen. His aspiration was to celebrate this enchanting, paradoxical land in a book. Eventually, Gifford and I met, and his passion for Patagonia was contagious. We resolved to join forces—his knowledge of the region, my photographic abilities, our combined experience of traveling in extreme places. Enthusiastically we began plans for a trip south.

For such a large piece of a continent, there has been surprisingly little written about Patagonia. I collected what few maps exist, studied the area's geography, and read everything I could about this intriguing land at the southern end of the hemisphere. Over the course of the next year, Gifford and I made many trips within Patagonia but concentrated our efforts on the area between forty-nine- and fifty-four-degrees south latitude. We chose to focus our attention on this region because it is the highlight of Patagonia. With an imaginative effort it is also accessible.

When I embarked on this project, I realized this was an opportunity to convey with images the unspoiled character of this exotic land—an opportunity to record the eternal wilderness that is an inseparable part of all Patagonia. It is my hope that the images in this book will communicate a clear impression of one of the wildest places on earth, and that they also will encourage an interest in this unique region and a realization of the need for such wild places where man is forever a visitor.

The photographs in this book were made with a Pentax 67 medium-format camera, which was mounted on a tripod for every frame. Lenses ranged from 45mm to 420mm. Warming filters were occasionally used to correct the bluish light in deep shade and under overcast skies. Exposures were calculated with a Pentax one-degree spot meter. All the images were recorded on 120 Fujichrome professional transparency film. Numerous photo locations and archeological sites were precisely surveyed for future reference with a Magellan 1000 Plus GPS (global positioning system) receiver, which was generously provided by Magellan Systems.

In making the images for this book, I was greatly aided by a number of Chilean people I met in Patagonia and to whom I owe a debt of thanks. In Puerto Natales, these include: Eduardo Scott, a natural history guide, for sharing his enthusiasm and a lifetime of knowledge of the Cordillera Paine region and together with his spouse, Lila Scott, most congenial innkeepers, for graciously opening their home, and sharing their warm hospitality and family between our rigorous trips into the Patagonian Andes and out on the pampa; Alvaro Vera, helpful, tireless entrepreneur, for always having a dependable Russian Lada available for our unpredictable travel needs, and for coming to the rescue whenever mechanical problems occurred in this remote territory that has never seen AAA road service; Mario Flores, for his effort in arranging the use of a most-scarce Zodiac for our most-unusual need for a boat on the pampa; and in Punta Arenas, Pedro Gómez and his spouse, Helen Fell, for sharing their enthusiasm and special knowledge of the Pali-Aike area and coastal waterways of the Magallanes region. To these thoughtful people who provided assistance and friendship—notwithstanding the language differences—and made my travels less worrisome, I am greatly indebted.

A special acknowledgment is due Carolyn and James Robertson at The Yolla Bolly Press, who responded at once with interest to the initial idea for this book. Despite the obscure theme and incomplete nature of my proposal, they persisted in going ahead with this project and artfully guided it to publication. Thank you for your direction and for believing in this idea.

My deepest gratitude goes to my wife, Louise, for her continuous support and understanding of my passionate interest in wild places and my earnest quest to express the value of wilderness through my photography.

And last but foremost, I wish to express my appreciation to Gifford Hickey who originally conceived of this project. Without his unwavering enthusiasm for Patagonia and the desire to share the place with others, this book could not have happened. Gifford's encyclopedic knowledge of Patagonian literature led us to the Chatwin and Theroux text for this book. Thank you, Gifford, for your unselfish contribution to this effort and your trust that my photography would communicate our shared vision of Patagonia.

There is a saying in Patagonia—*que asegura a la persona que come el fruto del calafate, su regreso a estas tierras*—those who taste the fruit of the calafate will return to this land.

I have tasted the calafate berry.

PAGE 3 I never tire of exploring sand dunes, of searching endless surface patterns for that rare combination of light and shadow that will entertain both mind and eye. Many localized dunes are scattered throughout the pampa. Winds deposit prehistoric silt and sand in the dead air spaces around isolated features on the landscape. Rocks, vegetation, embankments—nearly every object is an opportunity for airborne sand to accumulate. In this photo, native plants grow on a complex of head-and-tail dunes. Provincia de Santa Cruz, Argentina.

PAGE 4 Hurrying up the broad ridge on Cerro Rosado, I took advantage of each large rock I passed to duck out of the gusty breeze for a moment. The view was breathtaking from up here and exactly what I was looking for—a grand landscape of sky, mountains, glaciers—in these Patagonian Andes. From a shoulder below the granite bulk of Cerro Fitzroy, the frozen cascade of Glaciar Piedras Blancas tumbled into the valley below and terminated in a moraine lake. Upper winds smeared morning altostratus across the sky above the serrated crest.

Before coming to Patagonia, I read every publication and article on the region I could find. In one historical narrative, I learned about Salesian priest Alberto M. de Agostini, who traveled throughout the area from 1917 to 1945 and often carried a large plate camera on his missions. He made many photographs of indigenous people and places. Hauling his bulky equipment with him, he also made a number of ventures into the southern Patagonian Andes, brought back some of the first photographs of these unknown places, and became a champion for this wild territory.

Finally locating the precise vantage along the summit ridge, I sat down on a narrow ledge as much out of the wind as possible and pondered the fabulous scene before me. As I made several images of this striking cluster of peaks, I imagined the awe Padre de Agostini must have felt when he saw these mountain wonders close up for the first time many decades ago. Parque Nacional Los Glaciares, Argentina.

PAGE 7 For centuries, icy glacial squalls have ravaged Valle Piedras Blancas. These powerful winds have exposed this blowout at the edge of a beech forest and the root system of this noble beech—a patriarchal survivor of the harsh climate near the Patagonian ice field. Parque Nacional Los Glaciares, Argentina.

PAGE 8 A stream swollen by rainwater gracefully plunges down a steep ravine cut into soft metamorphic rock and disappears into a beech forest below. Foliated rock easily erodes along cleavage planes, as has occurred on this shale mountainside in Cordillera Paine. Parque Nacional Torres del Paine, Chile.

PAGE 10 Near the headwaters of Chorrillo del Salto, the views of Cerro Fitzroy are about as good as they get in the mountain kingdom. Studying a ridge that ran to the south, I envisioned a better vantage of this magnificent range. The weather looked promising, so later that afternoon I returned from our basecamp with bivouac gear and cameras to climb the ridge for sunset and sunrise photographs. While zigzagging up the ridge in search of the unusual, I discovered a shallow alpine basin filled with snow melt. It was precisely aligned and if the wind settled down, would offer a beautiful reflection of Fitzroy from its surface. I looked through the camera at the composition. It worked! I was hopeful of getting a special photograph at daybreak if the sky and wind would cooperate.

Meanwhile, a spectacular sunset was developing. Lenticular clouds had stacked up along the crest of the Andes and in no time were ablaze with the western light. The adrenalin flowed as I exposed frame after frame. Pink, fleecy cirrus streamed overhead. More frames exposed. Just as suddenly, the sky faded. Exhausted, I turned my attention to getting out of the wind and warming up. Nearby was an immense granite block that offered a protected opening under its lee side. I was soon snug in my bag and fast asleep—before there was time to ponder the consequences of this colossal boulder rolling over in the night. As dawn emerged on the eastern horizon, I backtracked to the basin and my promising shot. The morning sun finally broke through thin clouds and the air remained calm enough for this alpine reflection of Cerro Fitzroy. Parque Nacional Los Glaciares, Argentina.

PAGE 18 Macizo del Fitzroy bristles with granite spires—stone minarets of the mountain-shaping process. Towers and pinnacles of every size and shape punctuate the skyline here. Above lies the Andean-Antarctic zone—a world of ice and stone, and home for a few lichens. Brutal weather reigns on these peaks. I caught this glimpse during a lull in a spring storm that had erased the peaks for a week.

The first ascent of Cerro Fitzroy (3,441 m) was made in 1952 by climbers Lionel Terray and Guido Magnone and followed a route close to the sunlight corner in front of the shadowed wall, on the left skyline in this scene. Legendary British mountaineer Don Whillans and Franc Cochrane made the first ascent of Aguja Poincenot (3,036 m) in 1962, via a route up the snow ramp on the left shoulder, then followed the large crack system to the summit. Parque Nacional Los Glaciares, Argentina.

PAGE 20 Alpenglow is usually an occasional phenomenon at best. After several weeks in Patagonia, however, I noticed ethereal twilight skies were common in these Andean surroundings. Much to my pleasure, I came upon this delicate image one morning as early light cast its spell over the pampa near Cerro Fitzroy. Parque Nacional Los Glaciares, Argentina.

PAGE 23 On the eastern flanks of Macizo del Fitzroy, glaciers retreating from the last ice age deposited giant erratics on the foothills. These scattered artifacts now lie in ponderous silence like discarded orographic memorabilia and are a reminder of the geological phases that have passed. Parque Nacional Los Glaciares, Argentina.

PAGE 24 The Patagonian plains have preserved a vivid account of their geological shaping. Only a handful of rivers flow year-around across this forsaken region. Río La Leona, visible in the distance, is one of them. Many earth and rock features here suggest the dramatic processes that have scuffed and etched the veneer of these fascinating plains. Provincia de Santa Cruz, Argentina.

PAGE 26 Washed up by the last flood tide, a bleached conch shell reflects morning light on a web of mud cracks. Two times a day, dramatic tidal fluctuations on Patagonia's Atlantic coast expose broad mud flats around the great river inlets. Drying winds and solar warming create a maze of patterns as these surfaces bake and fracture until drowned by the next high water. Provincia de Santa Cruz, Argentina.

PAGE 27 Near the eastern shore of Lago Argentino lies a large area of shifting sand. The prevailing westerlies that flow over the Patagonian Andes encounter these dunes on their way toward the Atlantic. As the winds rake across the dune surface, tiny grains of sand are bounced along and piled into miniature ridges and in turn, accumulate into bigger piles. As if possessing locomotion, these hillocks of sand slowly migrate downwind. The dunes photographed here are of the *seif* form. Named for the Arabic word for "sword," which describes the elongated shape of this style of dune, they form whenever prevailing winds constantly blow from the same direction. Provincia de Santa Cruz, Argentina.

103

PAGE 28 In a cirque at the foot of Monte Almirante Nieto, talus piled into rippling moraines is evidence of the much larger ice fields that once occupied this valley carved out of rock. Everywhere in the cirques of Cordillera Paine, late-period Quaternary glaciation has left sharp features that speak of the youthful age of this compact range in southern Patagonia. Parque Nacional Torres del Paine, Chile.

PAGE 30 Torre Central and Torre Norte are two of the three namesake summits of Torres del Paine in Cordillera Paine. From our secluded camp in Valle Asencio, they emerged from swirling, morning clouds above a forested ridge. Their appearance commanded closer inspection. That's where we were headed. Parque Nacional Torres del Paine, Chile.

PAGE 33 Situated at the south end of the Campo de Hielo Sur, Glaciar Grey offers a natural channel for winds crossing the Andes. Choreographed by this prevailing flow, stiff bunchgrasses on an exposed ridge bend downwind, while far below, giant floating icebergs are pushed against the windward shore of Lago Grey. Parque Nacional Torres del Paine, Chile.

PAGE 34 Rising abruptly from the plains, the Cordillera de los Andes marks the western margin of the pampas in Patagonia. The rugged, serpentine crest—shown here at Cerro Fitzroy—is a climatic barrier along the icy realm of the Patagonian ice field, and to a much different maritime province beyond.

Until early in this century, Fitzroy was believed to be a volcano because of the clouds that continually veiled its summit. From a distance, they were mistaken for smoke and steam that supposedly hid a fuming caldera from view. The Araucanian Indians, who once roamed the plains of Patagonia, gave the name *Chaltén*, meaning "god of smoke," to this deity of the Patagonian Andes. The Argentine explorer and geographer Francisco Perito Moreno, who at the end of the nineteenth century headed the Argentinean Boundary Commission and was charged with surveying and mapping the boundaries of his country, named this cerro after Captain Robert Fitzroy, commander of the *H.M.S. Beagle*, which brought Charles Darwin to Patagonia. Parque Nacional Los Glaciares, Argentina.

PAGE 37 An epoch of glacial sculpting has produced this big wall in Cordillera Paine. Granite intrusions in dark sedimentary rock, uplifted during the mountain building process, are revealed in this cross section of an immense ridge above a cirque. The layer of dark sedimentary rock, which caps many of the mountains in this cordillera, gives these peaks their distinctive appearance and is characteristic of the strange land forms Patagonia is known for throughout the world. Parque Nacional Torres del Paine, Chile.

PAGE 38 The Patagonian pampa begins in the eastern foothills of the Cordillera de los Andes, the leeward side of the crest. These westernmost steppes of the pampa are paved with moraines and till left behind by the last ice age. Tempered by proximity to the Andes, and the drying winds that flow across the cordillera, tough, scrubby plants of the pre-Andean heath community struggle in the brittle continental climate. From these foothills, monotonous, undulating plains of Cretaceous and Tertiary sediments step down in flat-shaped terraces to the Atlantic coast. Parque Nacional Los Glaciares, Argentina.

PAGE 40 Below Curenos del Paine, lapping waves have sculpted ripple surfaces on these limestone slabs midway along the north shore of Lago Nordenskjöld. Reachable by a faint, circuitous trail, this shore is rarely hiked by visitors to the park. Gifford and I chose a more adventuresome means of travel to explore this area. In a small, collapsible canoe—ever wary of the frequent *williwaws* that could capsize us with little warning—we spent three days paddling and photographing twenty kilometers of beautiful, isolated shoreline of this deep, blue lake. Parque Nacional Torres del Paine, Chile.

PAGE 43 From a grassy knoll, this stately beech commands a view of peaceful Río Paine below. Along the lower reaches of this river and around Lago del Toro five kilometers downriver, rounded foothills are covered with perennial grasses and sparsely populated with thin groves of deciduous beech, comprising a distinctive vegetation community of the region. Río Paine is the connecting river for all waters flowing from Cordillera Paine. It originates on the north side of the cordillera at Lago Dickson, is fed by Ventisquero Dickson and the Campo de Hielo Sur, and ends when it flows into Lago del Toro. Parque Nacional Torres del Paine, Chile.

PAGE 44 We guided our small, inflatable boat into an indentation along the shore of Río La Leona and secured it from the wind. Close by, a low gully along the riverbank provided a campsite protected from the pampa breezes. From here, we spent the next three days exploring this wonderland of clay hills and basalt rocks. To our delight, the only footprints on the ridge tops before us were those of our indigenous neighbors, the guanacos. For our last sunset we climbed higher than previous days, up to a patch of bunchgrasses overlooking the clay landscape and this panorama of Río La Leona on the pampa below. Provincia de Santa Cruz, Argentina.

PAGE 47 Colorful pebbles, tumbled by glacier and stream, line the watercourse of Chorrillo del Salto below Cerro Fitzroy. This long, open valley is the main corridor for approaches to the Fitzroy basecamp and the peaks above. Because of the fragile nature of this environment and a tendency for visitors to converge on a few areas, it is also in danger of becoming overused. Side valleys and ridges along the way beckon the curious hiker who enjoys venturing off the beaten path and seeking out more unusual views of the area. Parque Nacional Los Glaciares, Argentina.

PAGE 48 Beautiful, miniature figworts—(Calceolaria uniflora) or zapatito de la virgen—take refuge from inclement alpine conditions beneath a fallen beech trunk. Many wind-toppled trees cover the floors of the Andean and Magellanic forests in Patagonia, their wood preserved for decades because of a lack of organisms necessary for rotting and decay. Few bacteria thrive in these harsh zones—key organic agents necessary in the breakdown of dead vegetation. Consequently, scant soils—with virtually no humus—have evolved for plants and trees to grow in, and only species that can exist in this gritty, decomposed granitic earth have taken root. Parque Nacional Los Glaciares, Argentina.

PAGE 49 At higher elevations, beech forests struggle to exist and are susceptible to destructive high winds, snow avalanches,

and, occasionally, even fires. These young beech trees are slowly repopulating an area in Valle Asencio in Cordillera Paine decades after an avalanche.

The beech forest is a stunted mat of vegetation at its upper fringes—a krummholz forest—as trees closely hug the ground to duck the fierce, desiccating winds. The krummholz line occurs at a relatively low elevation at these southern Andean latitudes, frequently being below eight hundred meters. Parque Nacional Torres del Paine, Chile.

PAGE 50 Under a full moon, breezes on Lago Sarmiento settle down with the advance of darkness. Landlocked by high, rounded, glacial-formed foothills near Cordillera Paine, this large body of water marks the beginning of the pampa in this region. As there is no outlet on this lake, the water level fluctuates from year to year (up to several meters) depending on annual precipitation. The alkaline water combines with calcium-laden springs in the area and precipitates out in peculiar, limestone boulders strewn along the shores of this natural reservoir. Parque Nacional Torres del Paine, Chile.

PAGE 53 The rainy districts up and down western Patagonia support vigorous evergreen forests and boggy moorlands. At some places in the Chilean channels and fjords along the Pacific coast, over five hundred centimeters of annual precipitation has been measured. In our cross-country travels, Gifford and I encountered some sylvan thickets so dense we had to crawl on hands and knees—often in cold, soaking rain, pushing and dragging our gear—in order to get through the elaborate maze of vegetation that had evolved. Parque Nacional Torres del Paine, Chile.

PAGE 54 As quietly as the growing shadows, the peaceful waters of Río Paine drift below Torres del Paine. We camped here one night on a canoe trip down the river to Lago Nordenskjöld. All evening we listened to the quacking and honking from up and down the river as our avian neighbors conversed and busied themselves with nesting activities. Parque Nacional Torres del Paine, Chile.

PAGE 57 In a symphony of whitewater, Río Paine loudly continues its journey at the outlet of Lago Nordenskjöld, just above the brink of Salto Grande. Río Paine drops over three waterfalls worthy of names along its circuitous course around Cordillera Paine to its conclusion at Lago del Toro. Salto Grande is the most scenic of these plunges and drops into a narrow gorge on a short stretch of river connecting the outlet of Lago Nordenskjöld to Lago Pehoe.

When I first saw this great patch of riffles, I immediately knew it would become one of my favorite scenic settings in the cordillera. Looking upstream over the cascading whitewater, looming Cuernos del Paine commanded my attention. Gazing off to the west a bit, the complex mass of Paine Grande takes over the view.

I've spent many hours at these cascades—some of the time struggling with wind and weather, trying to capture the special nuances of light at the ends of day, but much of it just contemplating one of the finest mountain panoramas in Patagonia. Parque Nacional Torres del Paine, Chile.

PAGE 58 As springtime advances, blooming firebrush—(Embothrium coccineum) or ciruelillo—cheers the scrubby, wooded foothills along Río Serrano. The entire body of fresh water that emanates from Cordillera Paine and nearby Campo de Hielo Sur flows down this broad meandering river. Carrying the outwash of more than fifteen glaciers and ice fields in the area, the silt-laden waters are finally consumed by the Pacific in Seno Ultima Esperanza, twenty-five kilometers away. Chile.

PAGE 60 An uprooted beech trunk, bleached by wind, sun, and cold, is now a memorial to survival in the harsh climate of alpine Patagonia. At timberline many of these trees appear as scrawny shrubs but are stunted, mature specimens hundreds of years old. Parque Nacional Los Glaciares, Argentina.

PAGE 61 The frigid, crashing waters of Chorrillo del Salto interrupted the dense evening shadows cast below Cerro Fitzroy. The means were painfully clear but the photo was obvious and needed to be taken. As I waded barefoot into the knee-deep stream, the icy cold water sent pangs through my feet and legs. Doggedly, I planted my tripod in the swift current, stooped, and

framed the graceful cascades now in my face. Next the waiting, hoping, willing the clouds to move away, all the while trying to ignore the numbing pain. After what seemed like forever but was probably only a minute or two, the clouds drifted off and the full outline of the peaks emerged. By now I was only functioning in slow motion. Awkwardly, I exposed the film and quickly retreated to regain the sensation in my lower extremities. Several days passed before memories of this effort faded from instant recall. Parque Nacional Los Glaciares, Argentina.

PAGE 63 Powerful katabatic winds—also known as williwaws—send billowing clouds of spray hundreds of meters skyward as they stream across Lago Nordenskjöld. Patagonia's topography is ideal for spawning williwaws. The southern Andes lay in the path of the westerly winds that encircle the southern hemisphere at these latitudes. These winds flow up and over the cordillera. Descending to meet the flat pampas below, the falling air mass behaves much like an avalanche, gathering speed as it goes.

Williwaws are commonplace on the great lakes dispersed along the lee side of the cordillera. Arising with little warning, the winds and immense volume of driving spray create treacherous conditions for any kind of activity on the water. These frightful, erratic winds gave Gifford and me many anxious moments during a week-long canoe trip, paddling Río Paine and its connecting lakes. Parque Nacional Torres del Paine, Chile.

PAGE 64 Living in the constant, icy winds and brutal weather near Glaciar Grey, this twisted beech tree, growing on a bare ridge, has become more than is suggested by its survival in hard rock and endurance of the elements. The weather it endures is also part of its character, an element of its reality.

The wind-battered, austere landscape near the Campo de Hielo Sur is one of the definitive examples of what wilderness is to me. I try to describe it to people when asked about the "wilderness areas" I've been to.

I've always thought that in explaining wilderness, climate should be an element of the description. It would then follow that the more wild the weather, the more wild the land! Weather is as much a part of the spirit of a place as the land itself is. Parque Nacional Torres del Paine, Chile.

PAGE 67 I've been seduced many times by a view of this trio of massive stone towers—Torre Sur, Torre Central, and Torre Norte. For days on end, dismal weather and clouds can make the sights and summits of these awe-inspiring landmarks inaccessible for both viewer and climber. Parque Nacional Torres del Paine, Chile.

PAGE 68 These sandstone totem pole formations on the Patagonian pampa stand as monuments to the great erosive forces of wind and water. They are the finest specimens I found while roaming more than five thousand kilometers in search of geological landmarks on these fascinating, desolate plains. Provincia de Santa Cruz, Argentina.

PAGE 71 Before the first Europeans began to settle in Patagonia in the late nineteenth century, Tehuelche Indians freely roamed the pampa. During the spring and summer months they would move up the wide, flat-bottomed river valleys toward the Andean foothills and hunt the large guanaco herds. These indigenous creatures provided the Tehuelche with food and warmth. Before the abrupt return of winter, these nomadic hunter-gatherers would retreat from their Andean hunting grounds and seek out more protected districts. There they would fabricate frail houses that were made of branch frames and sewn guanaco skins and subsist through the cold, dark winter months.

Gifford and I were determined to find some Tehuelche petroglyph or pictograph sites on the pampa in Patagonia. After several bleak, wind-beaten days spent stumbling up one dusty draw after another, it became apparent that the scouring winds and severe climate have left few traces of what sites may have existed. Over a period of three weeks we searched diligently, and were it not for a little luck, we wouldn't have found these hand paintings on the rock walls above an early hunting site. Provincia de Santa Cruz, Argentina.

PAGE 72 A band of sheer cliffs extends almost the entire length of Patagonia's coast on the Atlantic. In 1520, during the first around-the-world expedition, Captain-General Ferdinand Magellan and his crew were the first Europeans to see this cheerless feature of the Patagonian landscape.

After a trying day spent searching for non-existent roads, following dead end tracks, we finally parked our Russian Lada in front of the ripped-off door, on the lee side of a lighthouse. Painted white with three red stripes, our home for the night at Punta Norte looked like a giant candy cane sticking out of the pampa.

For a panoramic view, Gifford and I climbed to the room that houses the giant lens and gas-fired light. The *pamperos* howled at us with gale force. With every gust, the fortresslike, concrete column shuddered as the winds roared toward the Falkland Islands. The room was tiny, and the pressurized air whistled through every crack and seam, around the steel door and windows. These menacing sounds were accompanied by the *WHOOSH-sigh-WHOOSH-sigh* rhythm of the automatic light as it flashed. Four stories below, we were startled to see our car heaving and rocking on its suspension, like a tiny boat tossing in an angry sea of grass. For a long time we gazed spellbound at the sweeping vista below. It was all so simple out there—pampa, bluffs, the Atlantic. No signs of man. Not that we expected to see any.

Before drifting off to sleep I thought to myself, what a wilderness the wind begets. Awakened at one point during the restless night, we worried our small car would be pitched over the cliffs.

By daybreak the winds had subsided to a fresh breeze. It was slack tide, and we found a way down to the beach. I took advantage of the crystalline conditions to photograph some pregnant-shaped sandstone formations that seemed to be incubating in seawater pools on the mud flats. Provincia de Santa Cruz, Argentina.

PAGE 73 Ancient clay hills chronicle wind and water erosion on these badlands in the pampa. During a four-day visit here, we hiked back in time and immersed ourselves in these annals of geology. On several ridges were scatters of petrified wood chips. Far up one gully, we discovered a giant leg bone protruding from a clay hillside and believed it to be that of a large, prehistoric mammal. With fossilized seashells added to our findings, we estimated that these badlands date from the Oligocene epoch. Provincia de Santa Cruz, Argentina.

PAGE 75 Branching off the Campo de Hielo Sur thirty-five kilometers away, Glaciar Moreno flows into Canal de los Témpanos on Lago Argentino. This glacier was named for Francisco Perito Moreno, an early Argentine explorer of the Andes. Although small compared to the three-hundred-kilometer-long ice field, Glaciar Moreno is possibly the most active glacier in Patagonia. Península Magallanes provides one of the few, accessible, close up views of the only continental ice field outside Antarctica and rewards visitors with a magnificent show of ice calving across its five-kilometer-wide, sixty-meter-high face. Parque Nacional Los Glaciares, Argentina.

PAGE 76 On Oligocene badlands in the pampa, a colony of lichens evolves on a giant, basalt boulder sitting on a clay hilltop. Lichens are the fundamental constituents of organic weathering, producing the acids that corrode the rock-forming minerals. In breaking down rocks, these primary organisms play an important role in the development of soils but climate is also a major factor. Great expanses of sterile, glacial till cover much of the pampa in Patagonia. Cold, drying winds, which bring little annual precipitation, blow endlessly across these open plains and contribute to the scant edaphic development. Consequently, over many millennia, only an impoverished diversity of stunted vegetation has evolved on these arid steppes. Provincia de Santa Cruz, Argentina.

PAGE 79 Like pillars holding up the morning clouds, Cuernos del Paine and Torres del Paine ascend in stark contrast to the low, rounded foothills below. Such juxtapositions of scale and relief are a visual paradigm of Patagonia and a common spectacle in this paradoxical landscape. Parque Nacional Torres del Paine, Chile.

PAGE 80 Giant talus blocks rest atop moraine ridges in the cirque below Torres del Paine. For years I dreamed of photographing these magnificent towers. Now on this fair weather day, I sat for several hours on my granite perch and watched the endless play of light and shadow high above on the walls of these enchanting spires. These peaks have lured and challenged world-caliber mountaineers to their airy summits for decades. In January 1958, an Italian expedition led by Pierino Pession made the first ascent of Torre Norte (2,600 m). Torre Central (2,800 m) and Torre Sur (2,850 m) were both first climbed in the summer of 1963. Parque Nacional Torres del Paine, Chile.

PAGE 82 Like summer and autumn, spring is a brief season at these austral latitudes. But even on the pampa it does not preclude a showy exhibit of wildflowers, like this spirited display of miniature figworts. Provincia de Santa Cruz, Argentina.

PAGE 83 A beech tree bonsai tenaciously clings to life on a ledge above thunderous whitewater in a gorge on Río Paine. While making the images in this book, I saw and endured the moods of Patagonia—its stark landscape and raw weather—and developed a deep admiration for this place. This simple image eloquently sums up my impressions of this little-known land. Ironically, this was my last photograph of Patagonia. Parque Nacional Torres del Paine, Chile.

PAGE 84 Valle Frances is the largest valley in Cordillera Paine. Hanging glaciers crumble off lofty mountain slopes, and roaring glacial streams issue from ice-choked recesses below. While surveying the north shore of Lago Nordenskjöld, I got a close-up look into this valley and realized what a wonderland the ice age had fashioned.

Near the end of our circuit on the lake, we put ashore on a tiny island, two hundred meters from land, to investigate a display of wildflowers. I was happily occupied photographing my new-found subjects when, within minutes, a windstorm blew up. In waiting out the storm we were forced to stay overnight. The only protection we could fashion against the cold winds was to lie down in the cramped space between our canoe and a low clump of thorny bushes. At dawn we awoke to this marvelous view looking up the valley. Parque Nacional Torres del Paine, Chile.

PAGE 87 As a snowstorm breaks, high winds stir boiling clouds around the craggy ramparts of Paine Grande. Draped with hanging glaciers, crumbling, precipitous cliffs, and frequent summit clouds, it is a steadfast landmark of this region of Cordillera Paine. Parque Nacional Torres del Paine, Chile.

108

PAGE 88 A dusting of new snow accents the steep slopes of Paine Grande that loom over icebergs in Lago Grey. This complex, majestic mountain is the highest (3,050 m) and most massive in Cordillera Paine. Composed primarily of metamorphic rock, its summit peaks are interconnected by a large, broken glacier. This crowning ice field overhangs several sides of the mountain and erratically sends booming ice avalanches down the unstable, angular cliffs. Because of the unpredictable nature of ice falls, objective hazards on Paine Grande are high, and over the years a number of climbers, attempting its jagged summits, have lost their lives. Parque Nacional Torres del Paine, Chile.

PAGE 91 Throughout the austral spring, storm after storm rakes this region at the southern end of the Patagonian Andes. Rainbows—*arco iris* down here—are a frequent sight during this blustery season. Contrary to rumors I'd heard, they are not backwards south of the equator. This morning the sun broke through the clouds after a night of rain squalls and a double rainbow appeared over Laguna Armaga. Already, I thought, my first visit to Patagonia was exceeding expectations. But then this was only the first morning. Provincia de Ultima Esperanza, Chile.

PAGE 92 Laguna Armaga is an ideal place to see birds and, occasionally, even a mirror reflection. Chilean flamingos are often wading near the shores and feeding on the aquatic life produced by this laguna near Torres del Paine. One morning after stopping to explore the lakeshore, within minutes—appearing in twos and threes—twenty-three Andean condors soon filled the sky above a ridge. Soaring effortlessly and gliding along the nearby slopes, they no doubt were investigating the carrion potential in the territory or perhaps they were just curious about our presence. Within a half-hour, as silently as they came, they were gone. This is my first photograph of Patagonia. Provincia de Ultima Esperanza, Chile.

PAGE 96 Nestled in the wooded terrain near Cerro Fitzroy are several gemlike mountain lakes. Dominated by *Nothofagus pumilio*, the dense, deciduous beech forest in this zone grows snug to the lakeshore. Parque Nacional Los Glaciares, Argentina.

PAGE 99 The *pamperos* blew night and day for a week. We had bounced along for nearly a thousand kilometers on the pampa since leaving the more scenic foothills of the Andes. The wild winds sometimes helped push us along in our Russian Lada, but only when we steered an easterly course.

Our excitement was keen and hopes were high when Gifford and I finally arrived at this *bosque petrificados*. As the hazy sun dipped closer to the horizon, the winds grew even stronger and made walking and standing around a bit of a physical chore. The sky, already pitched to a rolling boil and filled with ice-age silt and dust, was beginning to look more ominous.

Minute by minute as the wind lashed us, photographic opportunities seemed to be evaporating. Anxious at the thought of losing another day's worth of light, we decided to hang around several hours before giving up hope and looking for shelter somewhere down the way. At one point I wondered if this might be what a nuclear winter would be like.

We renewed our spirits with a light supper of cheese and dirt, bread and dirt, all washed down with a pot of *café con leche* we managed to heat up—plus more dirt. Mealtime also included a few, now-routine interruptions to chase food that got away. Meanwhile, the drab sky slowly started to brighten. Shadows, hazy at first, began to grow heavier around every hill and rock.

I grabbed the camera gear, and we headed off. Soon the slanting rays turned bright and golden. Wincing in the face of hundred-kilometer-an-hour winds, it took both of us to hold down and work the camera, but I was able to make a half-dozen photographs of this primal, austere landscape. Monumento Natural Bosques Petrificados, Argentina.

PAGE 100 Cuernos del Paine (2,600 m) stands like a sentinel over Lago Nordenskjöld in Cordillera Paine. Though created and shaped by the sublime mechanism of orogenesis, the striking, black-topped horn formations at times seem to contribute a diabolical aura to this famous mountain landmark. Parque Nacional Torres del Paine, Chile.

JEFF GNASS